ADVANCE PRAIS.
*WHO WE LOST: A PORTABLE COVID MEMORIAL*

As this country struggles to grapple with the depth of
the pandemic's devastation, Martha Greenwald and her
storytellers open up the sacred spaces of memory, inviting
us to consider how tenderness and joy live alongside
unrelenting grief. This is a book that exhorts us to witness
and shelter the lived experience of pandemic death, and to
join in the effort to memorialize through storytelling.
In reading these stories we listen, and in listening
we remember.

—Sarah Wagner,
*professor of anthropology,*
*George Washington University*

The stories collected here, contributed through an
ingenious public memorial project, are the ones we all
know—beleaguered care workers, grieving families,
awestruck friends. It's all of us trying to make sense of
the incomprehensible things that really happened in the
first two years of the pandemic. Our duty to remember
is personal, but it is also collective. Memory is a gift
from the past to the future. This volume deserves to
be given.

—Scott Gabriel Knowles,
*disaster historian and creator of covid-calls.com*

# Who

# We

# Lost

*A Portable COVID Memorial*

# Who

# We

# Lost

*A Portable COVID Memorial*
Edited by Martha Greenwald

Belt Publishing

Printed in the United States of America
First edition 2023
1 2 3 4 5 6 7 8 9

ISBN: 9781953368539

Belt Publishing
13443 Detroit Avenue, Lakewood, OH 44107
www.beltpublishing.com

Cover art by David Wilson
Book design by Meredith Pangrace

"Give sorrow words. The grief that does not speak
Whispers the o'erfraught heart and bids it break."

—William Shakespeare, *Macbeth*

This book is for you—
The one reading the stories,
The one writing the stories—
May it bring you solace and peace.

# TABLE OF CONTENTS

## Medicine and Memory

# PART II: Give Sorrow Words: How to Write about Who We've Lost

# WHO WE LOST:
# AN INTRODUCTION

"I count myself in nothing else so happy
As in a soul remembering my good friends."
—William Shakespeare, *Richard II*

Because a book of stories about all the souls we have lost, and continue to lose, to the COVID pandemic would be impossible to compile, let's begin by remembering one man, Robert A. O'Connell.

Robert died of COVID-19 on May 4, 2020, in Queens, New York. He was seventy-nine years old. A month earlier, he'd allowed a coughing repair technician into his house to fix the furnace. After a few weeks spent suffering at home, he went to the hospital and was never again seen alive by his family, who feel as if he vanished. They loved him deeply—they always will—and his daughter, Kim Kuperschmid, finds herself full of memories that need to be decoded and protected.

Exploring her grief, Kim often writes and sends stories to the WhoWeLost website, a memorial space that I created and curate. When her narratives arrive, I'm reminded of details in a painting:

> A long time ago, our seventeen-year-old Basenji, Sandy, was very sick, and my mom wouldn't ever have had the heart to put her down. My dad told me that he took Sandy to the vet and had her put to sleep when my

mother was at work. (The dog was in so much pain.) Then, he returned back with Sandy and placed her on the couch so that it appeared as if she had passed on her own during the day while my mom wasn't home.

This act of compassion, something difficult undertaken decades before Robert died, implores us to imagine him waiting for his wife to come home as he sat in a quiet den beside their beloved dog. For Kim, this personal history is a gift; it offers a way to think about her father that is the opposite of his own ending, which occurred in an overcrowded critical care unit, among strangers, no daughter nearby to hold his freckled hand.

Robert's final days were similar to so many others who died due to COVID-19, and there are countless people who feel like Kim. I hear from them every day. They're angry, sad, lonely, and they feel that their grief is misunderstood and dismissed. The inability to comfort their dying loved one, to be with them, to say goodbye and then embrace normal mourning rituals, is a tragedy that haunts millions, and the echoes will be heard and felt far into the future.

The COVID pandemic had only been underway for a few months when the question arose: how would we honor those who died from this virus? Grassroots organizations and art installations centered on remembrance sprung up quickly, partially as a reaction to the swift politicization of the disease and the accompanying minimizing of its danger. Many of these projects were temporary, and some have ended, but WhoWeLost has persisted because it has evolved to meet the needs of mourners, most of whom fear that in the societal rush to forget the pandemic, their loved ones will be forgotten too. Every writer who sends a story to this project joins a larger narrative, and the power and strength of these gathered memories cannot be ignored. In the following pages, you will read the thoughts of nurses, doctors, mothers, sons, daughters, husbands, and wives. They reveal the heartbreak of final ICU text messages and abruptly emptied homes, but they also celebrate baseball, raucous laughter, and *arroz con gandules*.

I deeply hope this anthology offers comfort and fosters an understanding of what it means to lose a loved one to COVID. We must acknowledge that the profound absences caused by the pandemic leave no one untouched. Someday, there may be an official state-sanctioned COVID-19 memorial in the US, but even if it is eventually built, no one place can envelop our losses in a way that is personally relevant to all those who mourn.

While we are all living through the pandemic at the same time, I hesitate to call our memories "collective." Instead, I cite James Young's idea of "collected" memory as described in *The Stages of Memory: Reflections on Memorial Art, Loss, and the Spaces Between*, which asserts that each of us has unique remembrances of a common event that contribute to a larger memory bank that resonates differently for everyone based on their own lived experiences. His concept is literalized in *this* book because it is an anthology; you, as the reader, can connect with the collage of individual memorials in the way that is most meaningful to you.

So, a memorial can be a tall statue on a hillside, but it is also Mina Aguilera treasuring the image of her husband singing karaoke after a long workweek. It's Nicholas Montemarano's discovery of a Post-it note his mother wrote, detailing her symptoms before she entered the hospital. A memorial is Ti Spiller Phillips's remembrance of her son Kyle and their last Thanksgiving together, shared at a construction site while sitting "in green lawn chairs."

The writing of Kim, Mina, Nicholas, and Ti is personal and intimate, but their physical presence in a book with dozens of other stories helps paint a group portrait of pandemic loss. Remembrance is about more than remembering—it's about keeping memories alive and encouraging empathy while not overlooking or dismissing the past. This anthology enters that space carefully, asking all of us to pay attention to each other. This anthology is an elegy whose medium is memory, a memorial built of language rather than granite and bronze.

———————

"There is purpose in the telling."
—Dr. Pauline Boss

Mary Mantell writes and sends her stories in the middle of the night. Sometimes, if I've forgotten to turn down the volume on my phone, I'll wake to the notification chime, glance toward my nightstand, then wonder if Mary's insomnia is acting up again. Mary's husband, Mike, passed away prevaccine, and though she has loving children and grandchildren and is active in COVID advocacy groups, she feels adrift and left behind in the push to return to normal.

One thing Mary says *does* help is speaking and texting with others who are COVID-bereaved, and also writing down her memories and thoughts, often at 3:00 a.m. I am proud that the site exists and provides her comfort.

This anthology contains a selection of advice and prompts that specifically address the need to express grief through writing. All of the prompts are inspired by the stories published in this anthology. The stigmas attached to COVID deaths can have awful repercussions for those left to deal with the aftermath. Of course, writing is not a cure-all, but Mary finds it useful, and others do as well.

For years, researchers have been identifying and highlighting the psychological and health benefits of writing. There are numerous reasons why people report "feeling better" following activities related to writing about their experiences. Research shows it is not enough to simply vent one's emotions. Rather, it seems that a key factor in the curative writing experience is that one must write with an intention to better understand or comprehend the traumatic or disturbing event one is writing about.

This aspect of "meaning-making" may be a struggle for some in the loss of their loved one. David Kessler worked with Elisabeth Kübler-Ross many years after her famous work, *On Death and Dying*, was published. Their collaborative book, *On Grief and Grieving*, led Kessler to identify that many people yearn for relief from the darkness of grief. He notes that inevitably, grief will decrease in intensity over time, but it will never end or be resolved. The best we can hope for, he suggests, is that we are able to find meaning in the loss or transform it into something fulfilling, such as having gratitude for having had a person in one's life. Others may find that searching for meaning moves them toward new endeavors, connections with others who share similar loss experiences, and even activism for a shared cause. There is no "right way" to accomplish the transformation process; it is subjective, chosen by the grieving individual and perhaps influenced by their relationship with the person they lost.

The experience of isolation, especially early in the pandemic, is a common motif in the stories the WhoWeLost Project receives. Our loved ones were alone in the hospital, and desperately needed connections were short-circuited. Many have shared that the wound of their loved one's death "remains open" in ways that are markedly different than other deaths they had experienced before. Dr. Pauline Boss refers to this as "ambiguous loss," in her book, *The Myth of Closure: Ambiguous Loss in a Time of Pandemic and Change.*

Boss advocates that one thing we can do is write about our losses and "reflect on them." "There is purpose in the telling," she writes. "We pass on our narratives about the paradox of absence and presence, of loss and resilience, because we don't want closure." After corresponding with hundreds of people since the outset of this project and helping them write, I would add I've observed that very few believe that closure—as it relates to pandemic grief—is even a possibility.

They know they cannot undo the moment a loved one was taken away by EMTs or dropped at the ER entrance, disappearing quickly, as if being swept into a sci-fi starship. They will never forget frenzied Google searches to hunt for cures at 4:00 a.m. and the calls from doctors asking for permission to intubate or ventilate. There is no closure for an unbearable, grainy-screened final goodbye to your father on a cellphone.

In her book, *Writing as a Way of Healing: How Telling Our Stories Transforms Our Lives,* Dr. Louise DeSalvo highlights the effectiveness of using creative writing as a restorative tool. She notes, "creativity is a basic human response to trauma and a natural emergency defense system." She stresses "*what we write* matters." She suggests that individuals include concrete facts and authentic accounts with sufficient detail to paint the scene of the events and people who were significant. DeSalvo especially emphasizes the importance of linking feelings to the events. Through creative writing, she proposes that a person tells "a complete, complex, coherent story, with a beginning, middle, and end," which supports finding and using our voice about the events that have irrevocably altered our lives.

Many of the writers in this anthology, particularly those who work in health care, validate DeSalvo's theories. The trauma that they and their colleagues experienced must be recognized as an integral piece of our "collected" loss. They recollect painful events with clear-eyed strength and compassion, and they report that it was helpful to work on and share their stories—both for their own mental health and to honor colleagues who died.

Therapists Dr. Sheri Clark and Laura Jesmer, LCSW, both help facilitate people telling their stories as an integral part of the therapeutic process. They share that patients who have been impacted by traumatic events, including COVID loss, express that they felt "powerless as events unfolded." Writing has helped them make better sense of their lives in unimaginably challenging circumstances.

"When we write about our loved ones or *to* our loved ones, we keep them with us in the present—it is an act of loving connection," says Clark. No two stories of COVID grief are the same, though there are distinct common themes and experiences. And this anthology contains many stories that don't mention COVID at all. Instead, the writers choose to share nostalgic reminiscences, uncoupling the virus from memories of their loved ones. Mary Mantell writes stories like this, documenting small moments that occur to her in the middle of the night. I hope she keeps sending stories, whenever she needs to. In essence, that's why this anthology—a portable memorial—exists.

---

As the curator of the WhoWeLost Project, I review every submission before it's published, and I read each story aloud to myself. I come to this project as a poet and teacher, so my need to hear these words is instinctual, but I also feel this is a meaningful way to honor both the mourner and the mourned. In *The Sounds of Poetry*, former US Poet Laureate Robert Pinsky writes, "The medium of poetry is a human body: the column of air inside the chest, shaped into signifying sounds in the larynx and the mouth." "In poetry," he states, "the medium is the audience's body."

After a writer sends a story about their husband's life, for example, and I then speak their words, I have given their memories my complete attention. Indeed, the necessity of focusing on one story at a time was the initial inspiration that sparked the WhoWeLost Project. Throughout 2020, when Kentucky Governor Andy Beshear held frequent, televised press conferences detailing the state's pandemic updates, he presented a brief remembrance of someone who had recently died from COVID. Quarantined in Louisville, I watched every broadcast. The governor would become visibly distraught as he read the short eulogies, and I was moved by his compassion. It quickly became clear that the state's losses were growing and that his press conference remembrances, though remarkable, would still leave thousands of lives unacknowledged. We were asked, since the beginning of the state shutdown, to pitch in and be good citizens. I had several ideas about how to contribute, but nothing crystallized until, at the conclusion of one of these press conferences, Dr. Steven J. Stack, the state Public Health Commissioner, stepped back from the podium and gave a "writing assignment" to anyone who wished to participate. He asked that Kentuckians send him snail mail detailing their thoughts and concerns about the pandemic and promised he'd respond. I taught creative writing for nearly twenty years, and a gong went off in my head. I thought: Here's a way I can help.

While designing the WhoWeLost website, I came across a news item that changed the project's trajectory. The article described the existence of secret COVID grieving groups that met in undisclosed locations because the participants feared verbal and physical attacks from their family and friends. Most had been bullied on social media when they'd mentioned COVID as a cause of death. Their attempts to mourn were met with disinformation and cruel questions about comorbidities. Some were disowned, even within close-knit families. As I read what they'd endured, I realized that the WhoWeLost website needed to serve two main purposes. First, it needed to ensure a safe space for mourners to feel secure about documenting their memories; no comments could ever be allowed on site entries. Second, the site would house a "Writing Toolbox" that included prompts and tips to alleviate anxiety and gently help anyone who felt stuck or hesitant about writing.

The site launched successfully in Kentucky, and six months later, after being featured on NPR, I received multiple requests to create a national COVID memorial website. Most people who asked for the expansion said they wanted to participate because WhoWeLost was a website and *not* social media. As the sites have grown, this feature has become increasingly appreciated because, for the COVID-bereaved, posting about their loss is a minefield. If someone's grandfather dies due to cancer and they choose to post about it, they can expect the obligatory "sorry for your loss" responses. But if that same person posts that their mother died after a month on a ventilator in a COVID unit, they may be met with questions about comorbidity and vaccination status.

The hashtag "#notjustanumber" is a common social media signifier among COVID grief groups. The bereaved feel unheard and confused as to why no one seems to care about their stories. How have we wound up here? The term "information overload" is often used to describe the constant inundation of data from many sources that characterizes modern life. But I think we are also affected by its cousin, "story overload," and I believe this has caused us, as a society, to lose perspective about the magnitude of our COVID losses.

We toss the word "story," and the idea of it, about so casually. Commercial ad campaigns rely on it to sell perfume, pharmaceuticals, and cars. And, as it has been co-opted by Facebook and Instagram, a "story" can be defined as both an image of a kindergarten craft item *and* a truly important message announcing a father's illness. Swiping left, then right, there are simply too many stories to keep track of, and most of them have not even earned the title.

As cave drawings from 50,000 years ago make clear, of course, storytelling is universal to the human experience. We must return to that lineage and give it our attention because while we cannot change how or why our loved ones died, we can control how we remember them. We can rescue the notion of what a story is, as Mark Aldrich, honoring his father, William Robert Aldrich, does when he observes that sometimes it's vital to speak of our loved ones without the epithet "died due to COVID" and instead pause to remember their lives, as we do for those who pass from other causes. Mark asserts, "There is no right way to mourn or wrong way to grieve. It's never wrong to say I love you."

I pray that Mark's father was cared for by a nurse as compassionate as Jamar Wattley, who facilitated numerous ICU FaceTimes and writes that the calls were "often beautiful":

> you would see little children showing drawings they had made, newborn babies, families struggling to corral pets to look into the screen, and, of course, the spouses choking back tears, trying to say encouraging words. . . . I have heard the final goodbyes. I have heard the *I love yous*.

Read Jamar's words aloud to yourself, as I did, and truly listen to how deeply he understands the importance of his role. There is such beauty in all these memories living together in the pages of this book. We must write stories about who we lost so that we remember them, as well as ourselves, the ones struggling to "corral pets to look into the screen" to say goodbye.

# Part I: Elegy

# Hope, Heart, Home

# DAILY NOTEBOOK

During my last year of grad school, my dad was working nights, and we barely saw each other during the week. We kept a notebook where we wrote each other a daily note, often loving encouragements or a quick doodle or funny memory. Now that he's gone, I find myself flipping back through our pages to each other. Sometimes, I read one that takes my breath away:

*Happy Friday!*
*I love you so much.*
*We are blessed to have a daughter like you in our lives.*
*I cleaned snow off your car. Please drive slow.*
*Love always, Tata*

—Jessica Bostwick

# WAYPOINT

CATHERINE WRIGHT FLORES

*Catherine Wright Flores lost her father, Steve Wright, to COVID on January 4, 2021.*

In a jumble of dark and depressing data and numbers, there is still hope:

"December 2020 is shaping up to be the COVID pandemic's deadliest month yet in the US."

"Two billion COVID vaccine doses secured, WHO says end of pandemic is in sight."

"We've only extubated three patients successfully in the last nine months, out of hundreds."

"If we don't have neurological stimulus response in the next couple of days, we will have to make some decisions."

We fiercely believed my daddy—an extraordinary human full of wisdom, generosity, encouragement, and careful strategy execution—would defy those odds, would chart a course to avoid the worst of the conditions and somehow land safely, that he would recover and come back to us.

I watched a flight path just like that, not long ago, in 2015. My dad, a licensed pilot for over fifty years, began flying at age twenty, and in the months following my mom's heartbreaking death, he set his sights on helping others and creating memories in the aircraft he and my mom owned. He flew Angel Flight missions to ferry patients to and from the same cancer center, MD Anderson in Houston, where my mother was treated—his determined way in shattered grief of giving back to the place and people who bestowed time and hope upon us when a rare form of bone marrow cancer darkened our lives.

That evening in April 2015, he was flying home to Houston. I was late in my pregnancy with my first baby and wrapping up work and tasks, unable to join this trip to see family friends. Whenever he flew, I watched his flights on an app called FlightAware, a brilliant resource rich with information about altitude and airspeed changes, duration elapsed and distance traveled for any particular aircraft. FlightAware overlays the flight path tracking with the current weather radar, and as I watched his flight path delineate on the screen in my hand that night, huge swaths of yellow, orange, and the stomach-clenching red of significant storms ballooned in his existing path. Panic rose in my heart.

When my dad and mom were chasing bucket-list dreams in the waning sunset of her life with an incurable cancer, they upgraded the plane with advanced radios and radar technology for safety and efficiency. I knew he was witnessing the same weather I was, and I trusted he was fully in risk management and diversion mode, my insides inherently knowing his steady hands and unflappable mind would steer him safely back to us. Not only did I trust this, I simultaneously *decided* I couldn't accept any other outcome. Three months after my mom's death, the idea of losing him too was unfathomable and caused spikes of anguish to shoot through every nerve in my body.

In real time on the map, the bright green swoops of his flight path, reminiscent of a carefully choreographed dance, illuminated my dad's plane expertly moving a step ahead of the weather's path before finally breaking off due south to another airport (not the intended one, which was in the thick of the storms), where he'd landed dozens of times when we lived in

Lake Jackson years ago. The second FlightAware indicated he was on the ground, I was calling him; the line didn't even ring once before I heard his voice.

"Daddy."

"Cathy."

Tears of relief traced a stream down my face to my clenched bump of a pregnant belly, and we talked about what he encountered, his strategy, his worry, his pride in applying all he had learned in half a century of flight to deviate and land safely.

I didn't have to grapple with the loss of my remaining parent that night, but nearly six years later, in late 2020, the treacherous balloons of danger, this time in the form of medical numbers—oxygen saturations, blood gases, neurological stimulus response, pressor counts and blood pressure and heart rate—traced a terrifying and worsening flight path of sorts right before our eyes.

Each call to the ICU nurse team, receiving updates, my stomach clenched as tightly as when red swept over the weather radar in 2015. His embattled body veered dangerously off course and then held its position; a single steadier night gave us desperately wished for but all-too-brief comfort for a breath of a moment.

All of the strategy, adjustment, medical knowledge—both proactive and reactive measures—and just pure brazen hope and prayer—beseeching him, "come back to us," in the face of abject critical spiraling downward—were ultimately not enough.

The phone call connecting with my dad that night in 2015, the relief which poured from every cell? The phone call I received the morning of January 4, 2021, was every bit the opposite. The nurse's tone conveyed utter danger. Her words confirmed it. My knees buckled with the revelation he was near death and that we had precious little time to get there to hold him through goodbye. My stomach clenched to place an immediate call to my brothers and shatter their world with my words, the way mine was shattered moments before.

My daddy's precious life ended in our arms, my brothers' and mine. His last heartbeats thumped under my shaking hands as my tears traced a river to his hospital gown. Under crisp winter Texas blue skies at 11:19 a.m., a Monday, his soul made its way to heaven to join my mama.

It is assuredly not the last trip he would have wanted, the wretched unfolding of COVID. He envisioned a different slope and set of events, as if we can ever actually know the way our earthly lives will end. The trauma of it all looms large in my soul, in those who cherished him—and yet somehow still his purpose blooms larger, brighter.

To live for someone who cannot, to honor their hopes, to chase what they earnestly wished out loud for you? It is a gift. It is our gift now to make intentional and generous choices to honor his causes and loves. It is our gift to summon his spirit into our extraordinary ordinary moments and say his name under skies of every weather element. His spirit remains as present, as certain as so many twinkling stars in that dark night he navigated to safety. The stories, the memories in the thousands of flight paths of his life: a map to our lost hearts. A way back home to him, to them, to tell their stories and live and love forward. To hope.

# WHAT I CALL HOME

## Aszdą́ą́ Nizhónii Bit'ah níí
## Carol Curley Begay Schumacher

*Carol Curley Begay Schumacher lost forty-two family members to COVID.*

The pandemic has taken forty-two members of my family, but it has also taken away what I call home.

For indigenous Navajo people, home is where your family is, and in our culture, the definition of family extends far beyond the immediate. I have a lot of mothers, fathers, brothers, and sisters. And now, so many of them are gone.

Last summer, I went back to Chilchinbeto to acknowledge the losses and to be within the empty spaces, the empty places. I knew I'd be going home to a ravaged community, but when I left Sun Prairie, Wisconsin, I did not expect the experience to be so utterly devastating. In the past, when we'd travel to the Navajo Nation each summer with our children, we would take different routes so that they could see the country. It was an important part of our trip. When we got there, they'd hang out with their siblings, and they enjoyed doing the physical work—chopping wood, building fires in the wood stove for heat, filling water barrels—jobs they found fun but that are essential to survival on the reservation, and I made sure they knew this. So there was always this contrast for me—my life in Wisconsin after leaving Arizona in 1994, and the world of *home* when we'd return in the summers.

I was told many stories before I arrived, and I stayed for a month and half, discovering constantly how true and painful it all was. There is such remoteness, big spaces between where my family members live (and lived). I had to plan out my days with my brother so that sometimes we did something unrelated to grief. We had to do this to be able to breathe. The trip put nine thousand miles on my car's odometer.

You need to understand that the community itself has also become a victim of COVID. You see it the second you arrive: empty store shelves, deliveries left undelivered, astronomical gas prices. For some, there is no transportation or running water. There are tourists, but they don't wear masks, and they argue about the need to wear them. They don't see that we are just trying to save the rest of us. The reality of life on the reservation was always about harshness, but we survived our conditions. My parents' house didn't have plumbing for the longest time but was one of the first to get electricity. Years later, the community is still fighting to survive, but there is no acknowledgment from the outside world about what we continue to experience.

COVID exposed the vast inequities of our health care system, or the extreme lack thereof. COVID has blown up what little was there, and no one's physical or mental health needs are appropriately addressed. My people are left in the middle, having to deal with it, day in, day out, without hope or help, grief-stricken and left to their own devices. I have heard too many of the same stories about how a family member got sick with COVID, was taken to hospital and never returned; no one got to see them or talk to them again. There were no proper goodbyes, check-ins, or funeral services, no proper spiritual journey home, just gone.

Out of my eight brothers and sisters, there are two of us left, my older brother Irvin and I. I became a mother over all my brothers, two younger, two older, and a younger sister at a young age. And I want you to know about Hank, who I nicknamed Pundy Pun. I always felt connected to him deeply from a young age. He huffed cans of aerosol to get high when he was eleven, and I believe it affected his development. He never fully became an adult, struggled in school, and began drinking. He needed help and testing but, because of the lack of health care, never received it.

I noticed how he'd revert back to being a little kid, and I spent more time taking care of him, trying to understand. He married, and they had a daughter, but the relationship didn't go well and he was left. He always had a lot of loss in his life, and this was one more. But then, one day, when his daughter was in her senior year of high school, she was getting off the school bus and was killed by a drunk driver.

At this point, when this unbearable loss occurred, Hank was no longer drinking, but he wasn't taking care of his diabetes, and so he was actively losing his sight. He would call me and say, "I know it's dark out but I can't see anything." Hank lost his sight at age forty-eight, in 2017. He would be crying. I didn't know how to help. He was living with my mom, but then we lost her too and he needed to be taken care of. He didn't want to go to a facility in New Mexico or Flagstaff (the urban towns, a three-hour drive away, too far from family), bouncing from place to place, and he didn't want to come to me in Wisconsin. Because home is where our family is and he couldn't leave the place where his daughter was buried. He was tied to that land.

Sometimes, I would wake up to find he'd left me a message in the middle of the night, saying he was giving up, but when COVID hit, it made his isolation and emptiness more unbearable. In December 2020, he was still texting me every day:

*Yá'át'ééh Abii'ní Shaa díí* (Good morning, sister)!

Then one Wednesday, after he was at dialysis, I said, "I will call you tomorrow and see how you're doing." I called as promised, but he didn't answer so I left him a message. Then another and another. I called my brother Irvin and said, "Go check on Hank." By the time he got there, it was too late.

He'd gone to bed and was found covered up with his hand on his heart. He had caught COVID the week before and was dead those five days before my brother even arrived.

Hank was always lonely. His whole life. And he left that way. It haunts me endlessly. What more could I have done?

With Hank's death, I feel like I've lost my connection. At the first anniversary of his passing, I started saying to myself that he's still around because I feel his presence and I am alright with that. When I was home on this past visit, I longed for the celebrations and traditional feasts. We were a big family, and now there was no one to bring out the food or tell a story or sing. Often, to be safe, we had to sit outside my relatives' homes. Chilchinbeto is not the same. I felt the absences so heavily. Every day, at a certain time, I would look at my phone and wonder where Hank's texts were, until I finally understood they weren't coming anymore.

# COOKING WITH MOM

PABLO LOPEZ, JR.

*Pablo Lopez, Jr. lost his mother, Marilu Lopez-Santiago, on April 5, 2020.*

It was a cold cloudy evening, November 23, 2000, the day before Thanksgiving, a holiday on which my family would get together and share dishes—but my mom's were the best. This year was very different. I was 3,900 miles away from home, stationed in Germany, and serving in the US Army.

Being away from home, I missed many birthdays, family gatherings, and holidays. I decided to call my mom in Brooklyn. For her, it was early morning. She was drinking her second cup of coffee and having some cheese as I recall. She was always happy and excited when I called her. We spoke about how things were going for me and for her back home, but she felt something was wrong. She didn't hesitate to ask what was going on.

I told her I was homesick. It was my first big holiday away from home and our family and especially from her home-cooked meals. There were no Spanish or Puerto Rican restaurants on or off base at the time I lived there, but Mom came up with a great idea. She said, "Why wouldn't you cook a meal at the barracks and invite some of your close friends?" She said, *"tú sabes cómo cocinar y yo te puedo ayudar a preparar por el teléfono sólo necesitas comprar unas cositas. Si no puedes estar en casa, trae la casa ti,"* which means, "you know how to cook and I can help you prepare it, all you need is a few things. *If you can't be home, then bring home to you.*"

As the conversation kept going, I told her I was nervous about preparing the food, and she replied if it came out bad, I could throw it away and try again—never give up. I picked up my notebook and started to take notes and make a shopping list.

I was skeptical at first that I could find all the ingredients, especially pork shoulder, at the Army commissary. I reached out to a few of my buddies and found they wanted to get involved and bring a dish as well. To my surprise, I was able to find everything, even a foil tray. We got back to the barracks, and I tried calling Mom on the DSN line. No luck. I couldn't get connected. So I pulled out my cell phone and made a direct call from it. At this point, I didn't care that I would get charged thirty-five cents a minute because it was worth it.

Mom answered the phone and we got right to it. Here is the recipe, exactly how she told me to prepare it:

First, wash the pork shoulder with lemon juice and water, then rinse and pat dry. Separate the meat, pulling back the skin, then make deep holes into the shoulder. Put it to the side and start your mix.

In a bowl, mix 4 tbs of garlic paste, 3 tbs of Goya sofrito, 1 pack of sazón Goya, 1 tsp of black pepper, 2 tbs of adobo Goya, 1 tbs of onion and garlic powder and oregano. Mix very well, chop up some cilantro, and add 2 tbs to the mix. Now you can fill up the holes on the pork shoulder with your hands or a spoon, getting the mix all the way down. Add the 3 packs of sazón Goya all over the meat and skin. Place the pork shoulder skin over the meat and also season it with light salt and black pepper. Wrap it up with foil and place on the bottom shelf of the fridge overnight.

After being on the call for about forty-five minutes, I thanked my mom for guiding and helping me, and we said goodbyes.

The next morning was Thanksgiving Day. I got up around 6:00 a.m., took the tray out of the fridge, and placed it in the oven at 375 degrees for about six hours. Then I removed the foil and cooked it for another hour uncovered. At this point, the skin was nice and crispy and the pork shoulder fell off the bone, as my mother said it would. It turned out to be a great Thanksgiving Day with my buddies. We all shared a different dish and enjoyed each other's company, thanks to my mom. She was happy to hear it had all gone so well.

My mom had a special talent in the kitchen. I recall how when she'd make her pot of rice with pigeon peas (*arroz con gandules*) for a church event, the ladies would save her food and put it out last so they could join in after serving the congregation. Mom made sure her kids knew how to cook, and I can say that though I'm biased, she thought I cooked the best.

I treasure the memory of her dictating that pork shoulder recipe on the phone that Thanksgiving, or of cooking with her in the kitchen throughout my childhood. I remember making jokes and smiling—oh, her smile will always live on.

On April 5, 2020, I lost my mother to COVID-19. Not being able to be there with her in the hospital, or even see her, was devastating. My mother had no underlying conditions. She was a healthy sixty-nine-year-old woman. COVID took my mom but it will not take my memories of her and all the beautiful moments we shared. *If you can't be home, then bring home to you.*

# VISITATIONS

Nicholas Montemarano

*Nicholas Montemarano lost his mother, Catherine Montemarano, on January 15, 2021.*

A few weeks after my mother died, she visited me in a dream. She and my father were in a large space that looked like a school auditorium; it was filled with games and toys and many children. My parents were playing with the kids. What I remember most is my mother—younger than when she died—running up several long staircases, the children following her, loud and excited. She was light on her feet and fast and healthy. She led the children up one staircase, another, and another, and then she was gone.

My father—younger than he is—stayed behind to help the shy children who hadn't gone with the rest. "Come on," he said. "Follow me, it'll be fun." He helped the children up the same stairs my mother had climbed, even though in real life my father struggles to walk. Before he reached the top and went wherever my mother had gone, I woke.

———————

My son and I flew to Indiana to see my father. It was the first time I had been there in the six months since my mother died. My son worked on a LEGO with my father, and we watched baseball games on TV, and I was able to spend time with my sister and my nieces. But I went there, too, with tasks.

I wanted to visit the cemetery, and I wanted to go alone. I would go with my son and my father and sister too, but my first visit had to be alone.

The stone, which was being made in India, still had not arrived. In the grass above where my mother is buried, staked into the ground, was a small plastic plaque marking my mother's name and the years of her birth and death. My sister had prettied the plot as much as she could with flowers and a stone rabbit and a stone cat reading a book (my mother loved cats). I listened to the background noise of rural summer—birds and lawn mowers and traffic on the nearest main road. I sat in the grass above my mother's body, closed my eyes, and breathed. Then I lay in the grass. After five minutes, I stood. It had been enough time, and I knew I would come back with my family the next day or the day after. I didn't need a *lot* of time with my mother, but I wished that I had easier access to this space. We are a family that visits the graves of our loved ones. I wished that during any moment at home in Pennsylvania, I could snap my fingers and magically appear in Olive Cemetery in Elkhart, Indiana.

Back at my father's house—it's still strange not to call it my parents' house—I had other tasks. Maybe it was all one big task: looking for my mother. I looked for her everywhere. This was private work, and I was glad that my father was busy building a LEGO with my son. I sat in the chair where my mother slept at night, where she had slept the last night she spent in her home, though she had no idea it would be her last. I stood and stared at the empty chair and took in the feeling of my mother's absence. I wanted this feeling to break me.

Next, I went into my parents' walk-in closet. My mother's clothes still hang there. At the far end, where she must have prayed each morning, is a palm tied into a crucifix, and photos of her mother and aunt, and her as a baby, and me and my sister when we were children. I looked at the photos and smelled my mother's blouses, waiting for the acute grief I had come looking for, but what I felt was more muted: a dull sadness that my mother was gone and a tired anger that she had been taken by the pandemic.

Later, in the kitchen, I found a Post-it note with my mother's writing on it:

Cough
Wheezing
Very Tired
Slight headache
Temp 100.5 on Fri—Xmas Day
Coughing—appointment Sat
Listened to my chest—wheezing—X-ray—pneumonia in left lung
Quarantine 10 days

And *now* I felt more of the feeling I had come for, because it was *her* handwriting, and she had written this note when she knew that she was sick but did not know—how could she— that five days later she would be hospitalized, and two weeks after that, she would die.

I took a photo of the note, then walked outside to get some air, and that's when I saw them. At the bottom of the steps leading into the house were the shoes my mother had been wearing the day she was admitted to the hospital—New Year's Eve—the shoes I had sealed in a plastic bag in the hospital room after she died. They were positioned on the ground in such a way that she could very well be standing in them, about to walk into her home.

———————

A year after my mother died, my father visited me in a dream. Long after the pandemic was supposed to have been over, my dream-father had died. COVID had taken him too. His body was naked in a casket, as if for a viewing, except the casket was filled with water and my father's body was submerged. I could see him only from the waist up. He was paler than he is, thinner, younger. I looked at his face, at his dark hair. He was still. Everything was still. Not even the water moved.

# ALL OF IT WAS A GIFT

### Rachael Sandoval

*Rachael Sandoval lost her son, Keith Wisecup, to COVID on November 10, 2021.*

I can hear their laughter from the kitchen as I make rolled tacos. My boys are in the other room, and I smile hugely, happy to hear my children's joy. How precious it is. I'm thinking of Keith. He loved my rolled tacos, and his laughter was so gigantic it was instantly infectious.

I can hear him, but only in memory. It's my job to keep these memories fresh, to keep them alive.

Keith was the second-oldest of six children growing up in a single-parent household. My son was twenty-five years old when he died, and he had squeezed so much life into those brief years. It's like he was always bursting at the seams to try something new.

In my heart, I knew I couldn't tie him down. I wanted to put him in a bubble and protect him forever, but he yearned to fly. He experienced life with raw naivete, a passion that was so rare.

A song would come on the radio, and he'd be lost in it, singing, dancing at work and in the store. It honestly didn't matter where he was. I envied that childlike spirit in him.

Keith had Asperger's syndrome. Being on the spectrum meant sometimes I'd get those random calls in the middle of the night. We'd talk for hours. I think we both needed it. I would hope by the end of our call that he would have some social clarity. The beautiful thing was that this young man was actually teaching me.

He didn't let anything slow him down. Band, school plays, cross-country, OMUN, state spelling bees, skipping a full grade, DECA awards, three years of college, traveling all over, working two jobs—this crazy, ornery kid became *my* inspiration. He was strong and determined, but he was a momma's boy too. Together we took our silly selfies, jammed in the car, debated our music, and laughed so much our sides hurt.

All of it was a gift. Now, there are no more daily texts, messages, or calls. It all stopped when COVID took his life. I am his mom and I couldn't save him. No amount of mothering and loving could. My Keith was a vibrant and immensely beautiful soul and our world was a better place because he was in it.

I leave with these beautiful words from Keith, a message to me from his last autumn:

> There are few things quite like rolling out of your apartment at 3am to do a workout up and down High St, through the Short North, and past the Ohio Statehouse, an overall 7.9 miles. There was something idyllic about running past all those tall, bright city buildings in the dead of night before the rush of daylight corrupts us into desensitization. It definitely felt nice to de-stress because this was spontaneous. I was feeling anxious and high-strung about life and was intending to go to the convenience store for a snack to soothe my anxiety, but instead it turned into a workout and I'm glad it did because I now feel a sense of calmness and tranquility.

# WALK BACK WITH ME

## Dawn Hamilton and Ruth Ann Trobe

*Dawn Hamilton lost her father, and Ruth Ann Trobe lost her husband, Alan Noble Trobe, to COVID on January 4, 2021.*

### I. Pizza, Popcorn, Fireworks

The sun was getting lower in the sky, setting up for a beautiful summer sunset. My brothers and I had been called in early from our day of running barefoot in the backyard, playing games long forgotten. Coming in the back door, just off the kitchen, we could smell the popcorn as we bounded up the steps. Dad already had the popcorn in the big paper bag, which meant we were going to the drive-in. The sides of the paper bag had dark streaks where the butter had seeped through. Mom was pouring ice on top of the drinks in the bottom of the blue and white cooler, the ice making a clinking sound when it hit the cans below.

Dad was on the phone; I could hear him ordering pizza. I watched as he stood there. His skin had the summer glow from working in the yard, and his gold-colored watch was making the light dance on the ceiling and walls as he moved his arm. He was still in his twenties then, slender in his jeans and T-shirt and flattop haircut. I remember him then, just as he always looked in the early photographs. His smile, big with a hint of orneriness, and those dimples.

We drove to Sam's place on Shadeland Avenue, like we did almost every Friday night. There in the picture window of the small white building was Sam. The five of us sat there in amazement, watching Sam toss the pizza dough high in the air then catch it with ease as it whirled around down. Dad worked there with Sam briefly when he was a teenager. We were always eager to hear his tales about making the pizzas.

We arrived at the drive-in with the pizzas and parked our white Pontiac convertible in one of the spots. Tonight was different. Rarely did we get to play on the swing sets up by the big screen. Dad pushed my littlest brother back and forth, my brother's legs reaching high into the air with each push. I don't recall the movie we saw, but I can still see my dad with his arm around my mom sitting in the front seat. My brothers and I sat on top of the back seat with a clear view of the big screen and the night sky filled with faraway twinkling stars.

Between movies, there were fireworks. The sky was filled with long swooshes, followed by deep booms and colorful bursts of light. Reds, greens, blues, and purples exploded and filled the sky, reflecting off all of the cars, resulting in oohs and aahs.

I don't remember anything about the second feature. My brothers and I fell asleep in the back seat. I woke up as we pulled into the driveway but pretended to be asleep. Mom carried my littlest brother into the house, and Dad picked up my other brother in his arms. My attempt to be carried in by Dad didn't fool him. He reached out his hand for me to take and said quietly to come on. I slipped my nine-year-old hand into his and walked beside him. Just as I had so many times before and would many times throughout my life.

## II. Enters This Young Man

Let me tell you about the day that changed my world.
I went to play volleyball at the Community Center.
While I was on the court practicing, coming through a

window enters this young man.

Handsome devil—flattop haircut, blonde, T-shirt, jeans, desert boots.

My first thought was—boy, you think you're something!

He was.

We were married soon after.

For fifty-seven years, two months, twenty-four days.

### III. Dad's Walk

The light from the stove gave off a slight orange glow to the kitchen this morning, and the wall clock made a ticking sound each time the hands moved. Like so many times before, I sat there, so familiar, the quiet, the kind of quiet that happens when everyone is at rest.

It was 6:30, and my head was still in the sleep fog. I closed my eyes and waited, listening to the tick, tick, tick of that stupid clock. He was supposed to be tapping on the window by then to let me know he was there. The tap that happened right before the door handle would turn and the door, fighting the suction of the humidity, made a frup sound as it opened. Suddenly, the August heat would rush in from outside.

Instead, the only sound I heard was the half sob, half sigh that emanated from the knot in my stomach and the ache in my heart. Dad wasn't coming. He wouldn't be sticking his head in the door whispering, so as to not wake anyone, "Are you ready?" His eyes fresh and a huge smile across his face. He loved those morning walks.

It was time. I had to go, or I'd miss the sunrise. There was a slight breeze off the ocean, and I swear I caught a faint whiff of Dad's aftershave. The birds were waking up, and the stars were twinkling but beginning to fade.

By now I should be trying to keep up with Dad. He had such a smooth, confident gait when he walked. His arms swung at his side in rhythm with his steps, hands relaxed and open. The sunrise would color the sky in beautiful oranges, reds, and pinks, making the perfect backdrop for Dad's silhouette. The wind would brush his thinning hair, and the wisps would dance on the breeze. There was a calmness of his spirit here that the seabirds all felt. To them he belonged, and they shared the beach with him without reservation.

As I finished Dad's walk, I realized somewhere under that sand are forty years of his steps. His energy and presence left behind. It's still here, but he is not. Others had arrived at the beach by then, totally oblivious to the fact someone was missing. My steps were slower heading back, tears trickling down my cheeks as I glanced back to the ocean and beach my dad loved, hoping against hope that he'd be there, ready to walk back with me. For all the times I slept in or looked for seashells, I'd give anything for a do-over so I could walk with Dad on that beach at sunrise.

# ON THE ROAD AGAIN

Ed Koenig

*Ed Koenig lost his husband, Jody Settle, to COVID on April 19, 2020.*

Two months after I met Jody, he had his first attack of multiple sclerosis. He had been complaining of blind spots in his field of vision, and I had noticed that when we would walk together, he would drift off to the left. Now he was in the emergency room. One of his eyes had turned to the left, and he had an overall weakness on the left side of his body. The neurologist on call in the ER suspected MS, but it took several months for a definitive diagnosis.

A two-week regimen of steroids reversed the symptoms Jody was exhibiting. We continued to build our relationship, which now included an unexpected obstacle.

Over the next two years, Jody suffered three additional exacerbations, each one more severe than the previous. By late 1989, Jody wasn't able to walk any distance unassisted—he needed a wheelchair to move about. Besides the obvious, this presented new, unanticipated problems.

Jody's apartment was in a building that wasn't accessible. There were six steps from the street level to the lobby. Once inside, the elevator was too small to accommodate a wheelchair. This meant Jody required assistance getting in and out. On his own, he was trapped in the cocoon of his apartment.

For several months, we had been talking about moving in together. Now was the time. We found a fully accessible place nearby and started our life together. While this was an improvement—Jody could shuffle outside in his wheelchair—he still couldn't go very far without someone's help.

The solution turned out to be an electric scooter, which would allow Jody to get outside and drive around without assistance. Getting approval from the insurance company for the scooter was a hellish undertaking that only increased Jody's frustration and isolation. Eventually, the approval came through.

Jody's eyes lit up brightly. The necessary paperwork was quickly completed and the order placed. It was just a matter of time. "Hurry up and wait" seemed to be our mantra.

A few weeks passed. On a beautiful spring morning, Jody, all excited, called me at work: "They're bringing the scooter today!" Ever the mother hen, all I could think to tell him was, "Make sure they show you how it works." Jody snorted and said sarcastically: "You turn it on and it goes." If only it were that simple. Around noon, Jody called back: "It's here. I'm going out." All I could get out before he hung up was a quick "Be careful."

As nervous as I was, I waited for more than an hour, hoping he would call and let me know how his trip had been. No phone call came. Eventually, I gave in and called home—we didn't yet have cell phones—but there was no answer. My anxiety increased. The afternoon dragged on with no contact. At the end of the day, I rushed out of the office and headed home. I raced from the subway, only to find Jody sitting on the scooter in front of our building. He had depleted the battery charge. I could have killed him, but when I saw the giant smile on his face, all I could do was to laugh with him and tell him, "Next time keep your eye on the battery level."

That scooter helped to introduce us to many neighbors as well as several officers from the NYPD's Thirty-Fourth

Precinct. Once in a while, Jody would forget about charging the battery and travel until it ran down. If he were near home, some kind neighbors would push him and the scooter back to our building. Other times, Jody had ventured further. The first time I got a call at work from the Thirty-Fourth Precinct, I thought my heart would burst through my chest. All I could envision was Jody lying in the middle of the street having been run over by a car or truck. To my "Is he alright?" question, the officer laughed and told me he had run out of battery power. He was fine. Two officers had loaded him and the scooter into a squad car and were driving him home. It wasn't the last time that would happen.

The scooter reinvigorated Jody. He would drive the scooter onto the bus and ride to and from Macy's, an hour-and-a-half ride each way. He would head down to a local luncheonette, where he told me he joined the "ladies who lunch." And he developed a friendship with another neighbor who used a wheelchair due to a spinal cord injury. They discovered that they both enjoyed playing chess and would meet at the local park, set up the board on a nearby bench, and spend an afternoon with some friendly competition.

I don't think I understood what real joy was until I saw Jody on that scooter. I was a witness to the importance of independence to the human spirit.

Jody was raised in Texas and was a country music fan. Many times, pre-pandemic, when he was headed out on his scooter, he would wave goodbye and start singing Willie Nelson's "On the Road Again." On the days I miss him the most, I remember that smile as he headed off on another adventure.

# SAUDADES (IN MEMORY OF CECY BASTOS SLAUGH)

Mark Slaugh

*Mark Slaugh lost his mother, Cecy Bastos Slaugh, to COVID on October 22, 2021. One year later, on November 19, 2022, Mark's siblings, Charlene and James Slaugh, went to the Colorado Springs nightclub Club Q to remember and celebrate their mother's life. Charlene, James, and James's partner, Jancarlos, were all shot and injured in the hateful massacre that occurred later that night. Mark was not at Club Q with his siblings. "Saudades" is a poem composed by Mark to memorialize his mother.*

My mother always said there is no
English equivalent for the word
"*Saudades*" in português

It means the literal feeling of missing
Someone you love
And how can one explain that?

The closest word in English is "longing"
It took me years to equate that—
And still it lacks a certain something

Like pecan waffles, just nutty and sweet
Enough to make everything better—like her
*Saudades* can be a taste

That lacks the same flavor in absence
Of the ones we love. It can be
A feeling like the sensation of warmth

When two lovers intertwine or the
Unmistakable comfort of
A mother's hug.

I smell *saudades* in rose gardens
And amid pear trees and plums
My sister smells it in the perfumes

She left behind. Now that mom is gone
*Saudades* means so much more
Than the simple explanation in English.

I don't long for the sound of her laughter
I feel the *saudades* of it.
I don't long for the taste of her art

Made manifest in her food
I feel the *saudades* of her recipes lost
Like her life. They cannot be replicated

And the heart of the home will never
Be the same when I cook.
Holidays will scream *saudades*

Into my body, my heart, and my brain
And the twisting in my gut
And the hole in my soul

Will forever *saudades* the way
She made us who we are.
The force of the will she instilled

In making us better than she was
And I know that she lives on
In every kind word, in a number of songs

Which play the melody of *saudades*
Which sounds like a feeling
Which looks like ashes in urns

A lost body that once held a soul
Who personified what love meant
Because without that,

My mother taught me:
*Saudades* is meaningless.

# TRACES IN THE ETHER

KIMBERLEY MARTIN

*Kimberley Martin lost her husband, Michael Martin, to*
*COVID on August 1, 2021.*

The phone rings. "Hello. Is Mike Martin there?" "No," I say, "he died last year after contracting COVID." The female voice barely misses a beat, "I would like to speak to him about a Medicare supplement." In my head, I scream at her callous idiocy, "How could he *possibly* be interested in a Medicare supplement when he has NO BODY?!"

After tamping down this almost-outburst, I am incredulous that she's forced me to say it again, to restate aloud that my husband is dead. It hurts to hear myself repeat those words. I ask her to remove this phone number from her call list. Yet, brazenly, with not even a pretension of compassion, she resumes, now trying to sell *me* a supplemental Medicare policy. In shock at her coldness, I exclaim, "I don't even *have* Medicare yet!" Deep down, I want to demand an answer from her: "How can you be so persistent after hearing that my beloved life partner is gone?" Yet she's just reading a screen. Databases carry so many threads of all our lives, of Mike's life, separated from who is alive, who is dead. Somehow, these computers, even with all their programming, fail to comprehend the meaning of the bits and bytes that comprised my beloved's electronic obituary.

———

I pick up the mail a mile from our house down the gravel road. As you would expect, my mailbox often contains meaningful items like a kindhearted condolence card, packages, a local weekly newspaper on Wednesdays . . . but today all the mail has his name on it: Mike Martin. There is a magazine renewal, a recall notice about the truck, his national park membership, more Medicare-related ads, a bunch of dumb *alphabet* mail—AARP, NRA, AAA. All these envelopes addressed to him. Do advertisers irrationally believe the deceased recipient can see their messages from the other side? If only they were right. I so wish I could send a letter and receive one back from him. So much mail still being addressed to my late husband at sixteen months post-COVID settles it; on unseen server farms, in distant databases, in the dots and dashes, Mike Martin lives on.

———————

Google Photos thinks you are still here, Mike. I just got an alert. The app shows me its collage of "Moments Together," you and me. Highlights of our special trips. Montages of mundane moments. Mike Martin and Kimberley Martin. What was probably our last on purpose *together* photo taken on our wedding anniversary in 2020, the time *before*, when we still saw no end to our future together. I hope you could see from heaven that I'd scheduled your memorial on what would have been our next wedding anniversary, two weeks after COVID ripped away your life. I do have several photos of just you. I photographed and recorded videos of your final music performances at a local winery, and you singing for a neighbor's family reunion just before Independence Day, 2021. That reunion event was our last time to be out together before your positive test. That evening ended with us sitting side-by-side, exhausted from packing up your guitar and sound equipment, hauling each bag across the rough terrain back down to the truck. Beautiful fireworks lit the sky high above their trees as we sat together on the hard tailgate, watching sprinkling glitter lights fall through the leaves.

Google Photos holds onto threads of our life, even your last days. When the hospital finally let me see you, I took a few photos of you, your room, and the flowers and balloon I'd sent when the hospital wouldn't allow me to visit you. At the end, in the ICU, I took a photo of my hand holding yours, while playing music for you from my phone, trying not to weep too loudly, feeling deep in my heart that you were already gone. Finally, I had to let you go when they unplugged your life support a few days after intubation, your organs failing you and failing me. All hope abandoned us in that ultimate moment; the final photo I could take of you was not *you* but your COVID-ravaged remains after your heart's last beat.

# DOG BOY AND HOLIDAY GUY

## Ti Spiller Phillips

*Ti Spiller Phillips lost her son, Kyle Spiller, to COVID on April 6, 2021.*

When my beloved son Kyle was little, we called him Dog Boy. If there was a dog within a half mile, Kyle would find it and love on it. I've never seen anyone so in love with dogs! We had many dogs over the years, so there were many opportunities to give and receive love. Sadly, due to family chaos during his childhood, I had to rehome the two dogs he had come to think of as his own. I know that Daisy, a black basset hound-border collie mix, and Duffy, a white rough-coat Jack Russell terrier, met him when he crossed over April 6, 2021, at 8:49 p.m. He was thirty-eight and had been married only two years.

Kyle was an interesting combination of steadfast loyalty, cranky impatience, infectious laughter, and endless forgiveness. He could be crabby and intolerant. He was willing to be understanding and forgiving. At his memorial, one of his buddies said he didn't think he'd ever seen Kyle without a smile on his face. At six-foot-two, 390 pounds, he was big in every way. Big heart, big appetite, big smarts, big beard, big love.

Kyle was our holiday maker. He refused to let a holiday go by without a get together. The only one we missed was Christmas 2020 because I was just too nervous about the virus. But that Thanksgiving we had a big meal in the living room of our half-finished house. Bare gray block walls, a late November Colorado breeze blowing through the many openings yet to be filled with windows and doors, a football game on the TV, a microwave to reheat the quickly cooling food—a memorable day to say the least. We sat across the room from each other in green lawn chairs, Mike and I on one side, Kyle and Charlotte on the other. But we were together, and that's what mattered to Kyle.

Kyle had a natural facility for sport and language, and he became fluent in Spanish for his LDS mission to New Jersey. He played multiple sports and mimicked any accent, frequently making folks laugh with this talent. With the help of the church and his LDS family, he reinvented himself in high school and created a good life with his conversion. Although he drifted away from the church in recent years, he maintained the many rich relationships he had made. Some of these wonderful people made possible his outdoor celebration of life when we were too deep in our grief to do anything, and many more came to share memories of him on that bright May afternoon.

Kyle and I butted heads quite a bit through the years. There were plenty of times when we were both tough to love. But we forged some kind of loving truce and really enjoyed our time together. Strangely, now that he is dead, we have an even better relationship. We talk every day, though it is brief. He encourages me to stick out this human life, even without him. I miss his laugh and his generosity and his hugs and his genuine positive regard for us. He taught me to look for joy, though that is not my first inclination.

Kyle's illness lasted just seventeen days from beginning to end. He and Charlotte could not afford medical insurance, yet he was given every available treatment. We are forever grateful to his nurses, doctors, respiratory therapists, and financial aid counselors for their unflagging efforts to help him.

We have been together in many lifetimes, and I look forward to seeing you again, Kylie, on the other side of the veil. Love you, Honey. See you in a while. Kiss those doggies for me.

# SAYING I MISS YOU IS NOT ENOUGH

Clara Martinez

*Clara Martinez lost her son, Donovan Kittell, to COVID on September 29, 2021.*

## I. Heartbroken

Donovan was my firstborn. He came into this world a month earlier than his due date. He looked like a little baby bird. Then, two weeks later, he was my little Michelin baby. He was so very chunky and beautiful.

I cannot fathom living this way anymore. One moment I am almost OK, and then reality hits that Donovan died from COVID. He is never coming back. He was a young man—thirty-one years old. A healthy young man. (This happens multiple times a day.)

I see posts and messages and news on the TV and on the radio: *it's just a cold, it only affects 1 percent, COVID isn't real, you can't make me wear a mask, they don't work, my body, my choice, go ahead and live in fear, I'm not going to get poked.* It's heartbreaking. All of it tears me apart.

Twenty-one days after he received the positive test result, I had to make the most devastating decision to turn off the ventilator because he was not going to get better. His skin turned gray the moment the air was stopped; three minutes later, his heart stopped. No last breath—he took that alone in the hospital before they placed him on the ventilator.

I have been told that stopping the vent was the most precious gift I could have given my son. I find it difficult to feel this way. Is that selfish? Yearning to be able to have him live even though he would have been brain-dead, always needing machines to stay alive? But he would be here and I would take care of him.

## II. The In-Between

When I hear one of Donovan's favorite bands playing on the radio, I remember the exact time he made me stop what I was doing to watch a video of one of their songs when it first launched.

In This Moment was the band; "The In-Between" was the video. He called me (Donovan would say "call me," but "call me" really meant "video me") and said he wanted to hear my reactions. Now, In This Moment is one of my favorites, though all their songs bring me to tears.

(I know how he would feel about me saying this. I guess this is one way to get it out to the universe that none of this is alright.)

## III. I Dream of Donovan on 10/5/21

We were running and playing tag; I almost got him but he was too fast. We were running between our house and our neighbors'. Our house still had the tree in front—I stopped, but he kept going into the street.

Donovan was almost like a toddler. Then, he was ten years old. He ran back toward our house chasing two small dogs—one of them was Carlos. The dogs ran up to our house, then Donovan ran back to chase his kindergarten principal. The principal ran toward their backyard, and Donovan went through the house to the backyard. I saw Donovan through the open gate door as he leaned toward the principal, looking at me from across the street.

He had a smile/smirk on his face. He was an adult. I saw him from far away, then also close up. He wasn't breathing hard after all that running. His hair was medium length and messy.

Then the phone rang and woke me up. I laid there, and it didn't come to me right away who it was, but then I closed my eyes and saw Donovan's face again and knew it was him. He was showing me that he is alright, and the look on his face said he loves me. There was no sound in my dream—just the feeling of fun, playing with my son. The tree and grass had color, but everything else was the gray color of the painting of Donovan and me that hangs in the living room.

Please come back to me.

# I SPECIAL-ORDERED MY BROTHER

## Camille Gregorian

*Camille Gregorian lost her brother, George Gregorian, to COVID on February 16, 2022.*

My baby brother died of COVID in February of 2022. He had gone to a dark place, and despite having underlying conditions, he adamantly refused to be vaccinated. It was three weeks of hell from the day he went into the hospital until he died, and I was afraid the whole time. Initially, he was alert, and we talked and texted. Knowing how distrustful he was of the medical establishment, I walked on eggshells as I gently encouraged him not to dismiss their treatment recommendations. He blustered but accepted them and was "holding his own" during the first week. But the inevitable happened. His breathing worsened, and his kidneys started to fail. Before being intubated, his last text message to me was saying he was scared and then a big red heart emoji.

Then came two weeks of ICU hell: days where staff did not think he would make it through their shift, fleeting moments of hope but always dread and fear. So many people prayed for him, but he was the sickest person they had ever seen. I watched this little boy, now fifty-seven, who was adored from the day he arrived on the planet, die on Zoom.

I used to tell people that when I was eleven years old, I had "ordered" my brother. I clearly remember being in the car with my mother and telling her that I was sick of my sister. "Why don't you have another baby?" I pleaded. So the "accident" baby—my brother, George M. Gregorian—was born and instantly became the shining light of our nuclear and extended family. Everyone has a presence, an essence, but George's was always louder, larger, and impossible to ignore. Outgoing, curious, annoying, kind, generous, smart, and up for anything, including allowing my sister and me to dress him up in girl's clothing and send him to return Christmas trees we had deemed too skinny.

My mother worked outside the home, so I took care of him. People sometimes thought he was my child. I was just a teenager, and in the late sixties, that was quite scandalous. I didn't mind taking care of him. I did all the things for him and with him that maybe I felt my mother didn't do with me, and later on, I realized that nurturing him was healing for me.

Christmas was so much fun when he was little and even as we aged. One memory I will cherish is of him walking into my home on Christmas Day about five years ago, wearing a Santa hat, arms full of gifts and with a huge smile on his face. He had five stockings to hold all his loot, some labeled with his many nicknames: Georgie, Bad Georgie, and Mazod (which means "hairy" in Armenian). I can't throw the stockings away.

My heart aches at the thought of Christmas morning without my brother. I recall one particular holiday where there had been a family disagreement. I was enjoying a drink to ease my nerves and began dancing and singing to "Party Rock." I am not a good dancer nor singer. Georgie took his phone out and started filming. You can hear him egging me on and giggling like a little boy until we both crumple to the floor in hysterics. I loved that we liked to bring out the fool in each other. Now that he's gone, there is no one left to laugh with me and at me in quite the same way. I will miss Georgie forever.

# BEFORE COVID, AFTER COVID

KIM KUPERSCHMID

*Kim Kuperschmid lost her father, Robert A. O'Connell, to COVID on May 4, 2020.*

## I. Sandy

Twenty years ago, our seventeen-year-old Basenji, Sandy, was very sick, and my mom wouldn't ever have had the heart to put her down. My dad told me that he took Sandy to the vet and had her put to sleep when my mother was at work. (The dog was in so much pain.) Then, he returned back with Sandy and placed her on the couch so that it appeared as if she had passed on her own during the day while my Mom wasn't home. Dad did that for my mother. And because Sandy was suffering.

## II. I Had a Dream That I Broke My Dad Out of the Hospital and Brought Him to His Favorite Diner!

Yesterday's is a diner in Floral Park near my Dad's house, where I used to meet him almost every Monday and Wednesday afternoon for brunch between my husband's medical appointments. There just happened to be enough time to grab a quick bite for an hour or so in between, and Yesterday's was conveniently located . . . and we had to eat at some point anyway!

Oh, what simple and well-worth-their-price-in-gold these times were! These were the most casual and loving conversations. At the time, we didn't realize how special these simple get-togethers were. Yesterday's was our place! We even had our regular waitress . . . who I caught up with about six months after my Dad passed. I ran in for five minutes to tell her what had happened!

She knew. She remembered my Dad. She gave me a hug, and we both cried. She knew how special those times at Yesterday's were. (I'm crying now!)

### III. Last Photo

Birthday outside on the back deck. This, a last photo with his birthday cake on March 18. He was independent and fine and had just bought a new treadmill. I never could have imagined in my worst nightmares that this would be the last time I would see him. He was my biggest fan. We shared a love for history, maps, and music. We spoke every night at 9:30. He was always a great source of unconditional guidance, love, and support for me and my brother, allowing us to make our own mistakes and picking up the pieces afterward without saying, "I told ya so."

He got sick and drove himself to a COVID test on March 25 but didn't get the positive results until April 3. He spent the rest of this month at home, alone with COVID, until he went to the hospital on April 17. He passed at 2:15 p.m. on May 4, 2020.

I miss our daily conversations, his easy laugh, and his presence in my life. There is definitely a new meaning for BC and AC. Now it means "Before COVID" and "After COVID."

# Medicine and Memory

# ALWAYS

James was a police officer, and we used the word "always" to let each other know we were safe. If I was traveling, he would tell me to be careful, and I'd reply, "Always."

If he was at work and something bad was going on, I would get a text, "Always," letting me know he was OK and that he'd call when he could.

It became our stability.

*Please come home safe: Always*
*Be careful: Always*
*Let me know when you're there: Always*
*I love you Always, JD.*

—Jerri Vance

# SPRING 2020

## DR. MAX HOFFMAN

*Dr. Max Hoffman was an anesthesiology intern in New York City as the COVID pandemic began.*

I look down the hallway leading into our unit, its walls now lined with paper lunch bags, makeshift cubbies to store our N95s when we depart home. Through the glass doors and beyond the adjoining window, the proud New York City skyline stands up against the setting sun. By the nurses' station, someone has written in black magic marker: "Fourteen North, April, Successful Extubations: Two." It's April 7, 2020. We're just one of seven, thirty-two-bed units. That number hasn't changed in days.

It hasn't even been five minutes since the decontamination team left the floor before we can hear the faint beeping of a patient's monitor, growing louder as it enters our unit, heading to fill the now clean and empty room. As an anesthesiologist in the operating room, you spend your days listening to that beep. You learn to trust that beep. You take comfort in it, a constant reminder that the person you're taking care of is doing OK. When its pitch drops, so does the patient's oxygenation, your first clue something has changed, and the patient needs more to breathe. Today, the beep I'm hearing is the lowest I've ever heard.

We're running out of ventilators. We've converted over half of the hospital into makeshift ICUs. We've stopped all nonemergency surgeries. There are now four refrigerated tractor trailers parked outside the hospital, a field morgue storing the bodies we no longer have space for. Just three days ago, New York City pled over the national emergency broadcast system for more health care workers to join our effort, repurposing its many now-empty hotel rooms to host those who answer the call. At 7:00 p.m. every night, the city erupts in applause, cheering us on as we change shifts, reminding us that despite what we see, the city still has a pulse.

We gather in the empty patient room, our first time together working as a team. I assume my position at the head of the bed, surveying my equipment, making sure everything is ready to induce sedation, place a breathing tube, and connect our new patient to the ventilator. Under normal circumstances, we would take our time. We would spend minutes before inducing, filling our patient's blood and lungs with as much oxygen as possible, a safety net should we be unable to place the breathing tube in time. Today, however, we are not under normal circumstances. This patient is out of time. Despite his best efforts in the emergency room, his oxygen levels won't budge past 82 percent. Normal is 95 percent and up.

He's rolled into the room, greeted in silence as each of us immediately focuses on the task at hand. He's gasping for air, exhausted, dripping in sweat. From the head of the bed, it's impossible not to see things from his perspective, surrounded by strangers in double-layered gowns, masks, face-shields, and bandanas. I wonder what it's like for him to see us go to these great lengths to protect ourselves from a disease that he has. I wonder what it's like for him to appreciate that yet still see us standing here, in his room, touching his skin, breathing his air, doing everything we can to help.

I lean over so he can hear me through my mask and shield. "My name is Doctor Hoffman. I'm one of the anesthesiology residents in the ICU. We're going to get a breathing tube in to help you. You're starting to get too tired, and we need to get your oxygen levels up." He nods and gives me a thumbs-up, unable to divert his breath to form words. I look around the room, confirming everyone is ready and glancing over my equipment one last time. When I push the medications, there will be no going back. If I don't get the breathing tube in fast enough, he'll die. Even then, once he's intubated, his odds of survival, based on current data become, at best, 50 percent. I wonder if he knows that, but I hope he doesn't.

"Propofol: 50mg. Etomidate: 14mg. Rocuronium: 100mg," I call out for the room to hear. "We're going to take good care of you," I say and rub his arm as the medication washes in. He looks at all of us and begins to cry, but before his tears can even make their way down his cheek, he's asleep. Only one or two breaths have been missed, and the monitor is already blaring, reminding me that his oxygenation is low, but I know that. It's already been too low since he came here. By the time I insert my laryngoscope to visualize the vocal cords, his oxygenation is at sixty. By the time the tube is in place, it's at forty. A few seconds later, the ventilator is hooked up, and it's at thirty. We stare helplessly in silence and watch. The descent into the twenties starts to slow, and at twenty-seven, we start trending in the right direction, our collective sigh of relief muffled by the whir of the ventilator working harder than it ever has.

He died just five days later from complications related to COVID-19. For eight weeks from March to May, we came to work. We took our N95s out of our paper lunch bags and held our patients' hands, guiding them through their thresholds: their hospitalizations, their intubations, and their deaths. Every step of the way, we did what we could to let them know we were there for them, to remind them they were loved. For those eight weeks, we celebrated what small victories we could, and we mourned the far too frequent losses. We went home. We showered. We ate dinner. We went to sleep. We went to work. With enough time, eventually, we erased that bold black number at the top of the nurses' station, and it became three . . . then four . . . then five. Then, one day, a bed became empty and was never filled.

# THIS IS ALL NEW TO US

JAMAR WATTLEY

*Jamar Wattley is a critical care RN in LaGrange, Kentucky. He has been working with COVID patients since the beginning of the pandemic.*

At the beginning of the pandemic, I remember watching the news and seeing the videos of other hospitals using whiteboards and FaceTime to share communication between patients and their families; eventually, all hospitals started doing the same. This idea was helpful because it condensed the numerous phone calls we got from families every day, and it lessened their sense of being shut out from what was happening to their loved ones.

As a critical care nurse, it was helpful to my morale to see the faces behind the voices, to affirm the amount of support each patient was receiving from their families, all hoping for a full recovery. Especially important was the patients' reactions to seeing their loved ones on the screen. Very often you would see little children showing drawings they had made, newborn babies, families struggling to corral pets to look into the screen, and, of course, the spouses, choking back tears, trying to say encouraging words.

These video calls were often beautiful, and they allowed patients to interact with their families while they were completely isolated from the world. On the other hand, each call was also a grim reminder of COVID's reality. When I got a COVID patient, they were already on a high amount of oxygen. Families saw their loved ones on devices that were forcing oxygen and air so fast it sounded like the patient was in a constant wind tunnel. They saw the patient physically fatigued, sometimes unable to talk or hard to understand because of the BiPAP mask over their mouth.

They could see their loved one struggling, exhausted as they tried to fight for their life but sadly and slowly losing the battle with COVID. And then there were the video calls with the doctor, informing the family there was nothing more to be done, the disease had severely weakened the patient, the lung damage was too severe and irreversible, and that the hospital was recommending a transitioning to end-of-life care. I have heard the final goodbyes. I have heard the *I love yous*.

Every final goodbye I experienced hurt just like the first. After I'd left the rooms, I felt possessed by the losses. My mind constantly wondered if any of the breathing exercises or ADLs (activities of daily living) had caused a patient's demise. Was there anything I could have done differently or something I'd missed? After being mentally fatigued from racking my brain and remaining overly optimistic with each patient, I was physically exhausted from working so many twelve-plus-hour shifts straight. I needed to block COVID out of my brain. So I turned to trivial stuff on YouTube and got heavy into *Pokémon Go*.

I had to so that I could avoid mainstream media and skip the multiple interviews about how fathers' relationships had improved with their kids and spouses due to the lockdowns—it made me too jealous to hear it. I barely had time to spend with my family at all, and most of my hours at home I spent sleeping from being worn out. I began questioning why I should even go back to the hospital; it would be just another repeat of my last shift. I was at my wit's end and felt defeated. I was a shell of a nurse, hoping these waves would end soon.

They didn't, of course. It's a few years later. Things are better, but COVID isn't gone. I'm still doing the work. I'm still here.

# WE LOST MANY.
# TOO MANY.

Susanne Howe

*Susanne Howe is an activities coordinator at a long-term care facility in Louisville, Kentucky. The people remembered in this story are identified only by their initials to comply with HIPAA regulations.*

I used to think I knew a lot about dealing with loss. Having worked in senior facilities for over twenty years, I'd seen many deaths, both peaceful transitions and not so easy ones, up close and personal. Most were predicted and allowed time for family to gather bedside to say their last *I love yous*. Those whose passings were unexpected were usually considered the "lucky" ones, as they slipped away quietly in their sleep. All were followed by some sort of memorial service or funeral, where those who grieved were able to share memories and say their final goodbyes. There's a sense of peace and acceptance that comes with the opportunity for ritual. The COVID that ravaged our residents, their families, our facility, and the community as a whole denied us those necessary mechanisms for expressing our grief.

Just the act of pulling these memories to the forefront of my consciousness is a painful yet cathartic exercise. In my mind, I see their smiling faces, feel their embraces, hear the old sing-along songs sung enthusiastically (if not particularly tunefully), and cherish those hearts that were filled with love and acceptance. They were kind souls who had survived much pain and loss in their lifetimes yet managed to greet each day with optimism and gratitude.

These treasured recollections of my "family of the heart" swirl in my head, mixed with the memory of hearing the fear in their voices or reading it in their faces as they fell ill. They were diagnosed with COVID and sent out of the facility en masse to hospital ICU beds or dedicated COVID units. Many of them died there among strangers, with no family to comfort them or hold their hands. Those who loved them were robbed of the opportunity to say those goodbyes or *I love yous* in person. This story is my way of remembering these lovely souls.

Two of my "BFFs" were African American women in their eighties. We became close almost immediately—kindred spirits, I suppose. Neither of them cared that my skin color wasn't dark like theirs or that we came from different generations and frames of reference.

"G" had a tremendous spirit despite having lived a life filled with more than her share of suffering. She was always grateful for the smallest gestures and never took kindness for granted. She loved her family, bingo, music, a good piece of fried fish, and grilled cheese sandwiches. Compliments made her uncomfortable. I remember having to do a bit of arm-twisting to get her to attend a group art therapy workshop because she didn't think she could possibly create anything anyone would want to look at. The workshop leader had come up with an easy mixed-media project, and when G saw her finished project hung on our dining room wall, she was so proud. She started looking forward to the classes, and the walls of her room started to fill up with the fruits of her workshop labors. She thought of herself as ordinary and undeserving most of the time—I wish she could have seen herself through my eyes.

A mother of five and a retired high school teacher, "V" was calm and virtually unflappable, no matter what life threw at her. She was warm and soft-spoken, yet firm and resolute in her convictions. We talked about almost everything . . . religion, politics, racism, illness, loss, death, etc. I could always count on her to be direct and honest, pulling no punches. No matter what she might have been going through, she always had time to reach out to others. V loved Aretha Franklin, Nat King Cole, classical music, sports, and her four-generational family.

One of my best memories is a night out with G, V, and two residents from our personal care unit. My colleague and I took them to a concert by Black Violin. They were dressed in their Sunday best, complete with pearls and hats, and they grinned all night. We thought they'd tire by intermission and we'd need to leave early, but G and V didn't want to miss a single second of the show, including the encore. They talked about it for weeks afterward.

I first became acquainted with "S" almost ten years ago, when her mother was on our unit. S was special in every sense of the word. Although disabled, she was one of the most positive, giving, helpful people I've ever met. March Madness was her favorite sports season. She was a whiz at remembering birthdays, TV trivia, stars, presidents, first ladies, etc. Because she was so comfortable in her own skin, she never felt the need to criticize or compare herself to others. I really admired her for that—when I feel myself going down that slippery slope, I tell myself, "Be more like S."

These three women were there for me during times I experienced personal loss and illness, even more so than coworkers and some extended family members were. G and V had fought their own battles with cancer, and S had lost a brother to it. They were supportive and genuinely concerned about me when I was out for surgery and treatment, having my assistant text or call me several times a week to check on me and let me know they were praying for me. They bombarded me with love and encouragement.

We still mourn the loss of these and other souls in that awful week and the weeks that followed.

I will always remember "R," the career IRS auditor, for her self-deprecating demeanor, quick wit, and her "flying feet." She could have won a wheelchair race against anyone else on the unit without even using her hands. That tiny ninety-three-year-old woman could flat out move. As a younger woman, she had square-danced, and her feet never forgot those steps. When a local fiddler and banjo player came to perform for us, I watched her from behind, fascinated by the fancy footwork of some long-ago choreography she was reliving with every beat of the music.

"L" was a sweet Southern lady who loved people and music. She had played piano and sax for years and was the reigning champion of our Name That Tune programs, often guessing songs after just three or four notes. There was never an occasion when I offered a drink that L did not respond with, "Got a cookie to go with this?" Whenever I offer residents beverages, I still hear L's voice inquiring about the availability of sweets.

A Navy veteran of the Korean War, "B" and his wife had served as Baptist missionaries in Africa for twenty-two years and Mexico for twenty-one, retiring in the early 2000s. B was witty and fiercely independent, only coming to long-term care shortly before his ninety-second birthday. Up to that time, he would be off on his scooter, zipping through the parking lot on his way to the drugstore, barbershop, church, or simply out for a ride in the fresh air.

"A" had resided with us for several years. She taught in a one-room school in the rural Midwest as a young woman and was the master of trivia and word games. She had a vivid imagination and kept us all amused with her fanciful tales. Her sing-along song request was always "Mairsy Doats."

There were more, so many more, and my mourning here is just a beginning to remembering. Yes, all these people were elderly, they resided in a long-term care facility, and they were part of an identified "at-risk" population, but they were coping with their health concerns, had good care, quality of life by their own standards, and family and friends who loved them. They were not expendable. Their lives mattered.

Our facility was not alone, as there were thousands of long-term care communities across the nation that experienced similar losses. Some larger ones were hit even harder. There's a wave of burnout in health care largely attributable to the constant stress of loss and unexpressed grief. It's like a tsunami rolling across the nation. The beds of those we lost have been filled by others multiple times since then, but the holes in our hearts will never be filled.

# JAMES VANCE'S STRANGER

## Rebecca Pape

*Rebecca Pape is a cardiothoracic ICU travel nurse and army veteran. She lives in Pittsburgh, Pennsylvania.*

I selfishly didn't believe in the virus when it first made the news in December of 2019. I thought it was a way for the mass media to combat the drudge of the everyday shootings and to reengage viewers with a possibility to cause hysteria; exactly what mass media needs to reel viewers in. With each day that ticked into March, there were new provisions and laws set in place for this mysterious virus that was practically unknown to the US. I became angry. Women were giving birth to their first child alone, weddings were canceled, and loved ones who died were sent immediately for cremation, mourning with family no longer a possibility.

The hospitals grew more barren over the summer of 2020. Nurses were not only taking on their daily jobs but were now adding new titles and experiences due to the exodus of health care professionals leaving their jobs all over the world, giving bedside nurses an even broader-scoped definition of "jack-of-all-trades."

The first time I walked into the COVID bay in September 2020, I stopped dead in my tracks with my PAPR suit on and IV drips in my hand. I walked up to the isolation door and saw a large note from the PACU nurses who had packed up their entire unit and dispersed all over the hospitals into new wings so that our ICU could expand and bring in the more severely ill COVID-positive critical patients who needed us. All I could hear was the soft blow of the respirators filtering air, alarms on cardiac circuits, and my own racing heartbeat. The only way I can explain how it was is to invoke the moment we watched the planes hitting into the Twin Towers on 9/11. We remember where we were, we remember how we felt, and we remember the horror in our minds as we thought of every person who lost their life on impact.

I looked across the bay. Spread out were ten to fifteen ECMO circuits, each of the patients separately laying naked under one sheet with paralytic running through their bodies to relax, some of them lying prone on their stomachs with their heads facing me. Due to acute respiratory distress syndrome, many of the patients were on VV-ECMO, which is typically used for severely ill COVID-positive patients. When COVID-19 infiltrates the lung tissue, parts of the lung become scarred and fibrous. The lymphatic system floods the lungs with cytokines as a response to destroy the virus, which creates large amounts of secretions from the lungs that have a distinct look on a chest X-ray. These areas of the lung cannot perfuse oxygen-rich blood back to the heart, which creates dead space in the lung. Cannulas drain back half the blood to the lungs and send it through an oxygenator membrane to remove clots and oxygenate the blood back to the heart. The patients typically are on an IV drip that paralyzes the lung tissue and diaphragm and creates more expansion for the ventilator to expand the lungs to heal, while the patient is sedated because life support is traumatic for the patient who is awake and looking around. Every eight hours, all the nurses, respiratory therapists, and X-ray technicians don PAPRs and go in as a team to roll the patients from a prone to supine position for optimal oxygenation of their sick lungs. One of our attending critical care doctors bought us a Bose sound speaker so that while we were all in the bay, we could listen to music as we cared for our patients. I never thought something as simple as a speaker would have so much meaning.

My biggest fear entering critical care nursing was how I would mentally handle patient death and postmortem care. In the COVID units during these times, there were absolutely no visitors allowed. Loved ones had to say goodbye to their mothers, husbands, sisters, and children on FaceTime with the iPads the hospital provided us, as we held patients' hands and cried together. Once a patient passed away, we ended the call and started a bed bath for the deceased. We bathed them, dried them, and loaded them in a body bag. To get to the morgue, we had to call the security officers to meet us at the door in N95 masks after they cleared the floor of staff and guided us to the morgue within the hospital basement. I will always remember the names of every patient I cared for who passed away. I will remember wheeling them into the morgue, dripping tears in my suit and wondering if I was the last person to ever see them alive.

I grew angry and cold into winter. I was devastated for the families, hurt that I felt guilty to even go to the grocery store, and I grew furious at people who thought the virus wasn't real and that the death rates were a hoax. I would drive home in utter silence, windows down, airing myself out after sweating for twelve hours in my PAPR suit, hearing echoes of ventilators and heart monitor alarms in my head. When I came home to my house, I would cry again, thinking how blessed I was to hold the hand of my patients as they took their last breath, and thinking how lucky I was to be healthy and have my loved ones.

December 8, 2020, was when I met James Vance, unbeknownst to him. I came in to get report, and as I finished, the night shift nurse and I went to assess him together. I stood at the foot of his bed—ECMO circuit perfusing—staring at his calm and rested face. While assessing him, I noticed a Marine insignia tattoo, and I knew from report he was a retired lieutenant from West Virginia. I became indignant thinking of how this virus had no boundaries. A man who served his country, dedicated a career to fighting for strangers and protecting them, had been taken down by a poorly understood virus. It wasn't fair. Many of us nurses were paired with a patient on ECMO and added overtime shifts to our regular schedule to resuscitate patients and fight for them to go home one day. I distinctly remember one afternoon when all the teams came in for prone-supining, he opened his eyes and looked around and locked eyes with me. His stranger. I rubbed his head in my double-gloved hand and came in close to him so he could hear me through my suit. "Mr. Vance, you are here at Allegheny General Hospital, your lungs are very sick. We are keeping you asleep to rest your lungs and help you recover. You will never, ever be alone, there are ten nurses here at all times watching you. Your wife and family have called twice a day to get updates on you. They know you are here and we are going to fight to get you out of here and get you home to them." With a soft nod of acknowledgement, he drifted back to sleep.

January 2, 2021, I was sitting in the break room warming up my lunch, and a nurse that had also cared for James came in and said, "Becca . . . did you hear about James Vance?" I looked up from my phone and into her welled eyes as she said, "He passed away in MICU yesterday." Without a single word said after that sentence, we both looked at each other and cried. The absolute exhaustion on our faces poured from our eyes.

From that day forward, I realized that I was clenching my teeth in my sleep, gripping the steering wheel a little too hard after driving home from work, staring at a single tile in the shower as I let the hot water pour over me, hoping it would burn any bacteria or virus I carried home. I stopped going out. I wasn't scared; I was angry, I was heartbroken, I hurt.

Throughout the winter, I sunk into the right side of my couch, practically making a body imprint. No one I knew outside of the ECMO ICU understood how devastating it felt to be off work just a few days and come back to see empty beds or beds with fresh new patients on fresh new ECMO circuits from new states. Looking back in hindsight, every single day in that bay chipped at my heart, opening me to post-traumatic stress.

I can remember standing next to the toughest nurse I worked with as she opened the iPad and answered the last FaceTime call for her patient's family so they could lay eyes on their dad and give him their final goodbye. I looked at her face through the plastic cape and watched the tears pour from her eyes in one blink as she said, "I can't do this anymore. This is killing me." I knew I could finally admit to my coworkers how raw and empty I was. There is a mindset in cardiothoracic ICU that you must be mentally tough to do your job. You cannot let death and illness affect you because carrying that load will affect how you perform. I didn't care anymore; it was time I unloaded and told someone how I felt.

I left work that morning and called the Pittsburgh VA mental health hotline. I told them I couldn't bear looking death in the face anymore. I couldn't bear knowing that families wait around the phone at home for a call of bad news. I couldn't bear knowing that my amazing angelic coworkers and me were losing themselves. So I came into the emergency room begging for help. I wasn't sure what to do or where to go, but I knew I couldn't be alone with my mind another day.

Then I met Jerri, James Vance's wife. Jerri and I had remembered each other from update phone calls each shift. Before James survived ECMO decannulation and was transferred to another ICU for rehabilitation, I was able to update Jerri that he was looking amazing; all the numbers we trend every few hours had looked the best we had hoped for. The last day I had James, I drove home knowing I had made a lifetime impact on him and his family in some way. I felt good: all those lonely sleepless nights were worth it. Little did I know that the lifetime impact on his family would not be what I imagined. Now I found myself reaching out to her to mourn her husband.

Jerri and I stayed in touch through text for longer than a year. It was easy to talk to my stranger. She understood the most. I knew James, but I had no idea who James was. I felt embarrassed to admit how much his sudden death affected me because I had worked so hard to resuscitate him. It goes to show that in life, we never know when our time will come. Getting those "You can do this" texts from a widow who was raising her family alone, all while mourning the loss of her husband, felt wrong at first. But the more we talked and got to know each other, the more Jerri became my sister.

In April 2022, we finally met in person. Jerri brought her gorgeous daughters Jamie and Julie with her. We met at an ice cream shop in downtown Pittsburgh late at night. I pulled into my parking spot and gulped. I was scared to see her and break down or not have the words to sympathize with her, because the reality of her situation is that there *aren't* words to help her.

As we walked into the shop, I looked back toward them and saw their little faces—carbon copies of my stranger I'd fought to keep alive. I was going to write that I never knew James, but that would be a lie. I knew him in a different way than his wife and family knew him. I knew him as helpless, depending on the strength of his strangers to keep him alive—in a different light than he had lived his entire life. I knew his eyes, lips, and eyebrows. As I stared at his girls and their smirks, as I poorly tried to crack jokes, I felt a frog form in my throat. I saw his eyes, lips, and eyebrows in his little girls. What a beautiful thing it was for me, at thirty years old, to realize that we live on in our children.

Jerri and I are sisters. December 8 and January 1 hold differently to me now. Working nearly every holiday at bedside with strangers over the last ten years has taught me that holidays mean nothing; it's who we spend our lives with on a random Tuesday, it's the cards we receive in the mail from old friends during a pandemic saying, "Just thinking of you." It's leaving work at 8:00 p.m. and watching strangers on the sidewalk clap for you to show how meaningful your work is to them. It's a new lifelong sisterhood that should be celebrated. Millie's Ice Cream Shop, April 17, 2022, is a moment in time that no virus will steal from us.

# WHO WE LOST

## Steven J. Stack, MD, MBA

*Dr. Stack was appointed as commissioner of the Kentucky Department for Public Health in February 2020, just one month before the pandemic began in the state.*

The early days were harrowing and uncertain. In December 2019, critically ill patients afflicted with an unknown pathogen swept through China's Wuhan province, overwhelming hospitals and rapidly outstripping ICU and ventilator resources. By February 2020, Northern Italy endured a similar crisis, and infected patients appeared throughout the world, including Kentucky, on March 6.

SARS-CoV-2, aka COVID-19, had swept across the globe with breakneck speed to imperil all of humanity. No one on earth had immunity, diagnostic tests were scarce, medical protective equipment was unavailable, specific treatments were unknown, and preventive vaccinations were nonexistent. Early modeling estimated 1 to 2 percent of all persons infected might die—potentially 45,000 to 90,000 Kentuckians.

In the weeks and months that followed, 4.5 million Kentuckians joined all of humanity in a breathtaking, all-of-society response to a global infectious threat of biblical proportions. Statewide and national testing networks were created. Personal protective equipment was globally sourced. Novel and scarce medical treatments were produced and apportioned. And lifesaving vaccines were developed, distributed, and administered at an astonishing speed and scale to many who wept tears of relief upon receiving them. Throughout this journey, Kentuckians transitioned through Healthy at Home, Healthy at Work, a record-setting vaccination campaign, and multiple surges (e.g., alpha, delta, and omicron) that brought our healers and hospitals to the point of collapse. Each one of us preserves lifelong memories of these generation-defining historic events.

After more than two and a half years, humanity hopes to have reached the "living with COVID" phase in which vaccines and narrowly targeted interventions enable society to return to a sustainable sense of normalcy. The disease, though, having already claimed the lives of nearly 17,000 Kentuckians and more than one million Americans, declines to release us, and we refuse to let it define us—a détente with the destroyer.

We learned a lot about each other. Through compassion and caring for each other, we could flatten the curve. Green lights across the commonwealth honored the fallen and inspired the remaining to preserve hope that better days would return. Daily 5:00 p.m. briefings pulled Kentuckians together, proving that what unites us can overcome what divides us if we choose. One day and one small act of kindness at a time, we showed that we could get through this and we would get through this together.

Being Kentucky's commissioner for public health during the pandemic has many times been difficult but has always been a privilege—every day of it. Standing beside Governor Beshear in service to our fellow Kentuckians through these difficult times has been an honor of a lifetime. As I reflect on those we have lost, I remain mindful of the many saved and the power we possess to overcome adversity when we choose to see our neighbors as friends, not adversaries. Our greatest power, perhaps, has always been our individual choices to be kind and caring to each other.

# WHAT WOULD GARY DO?

Jacqueline H. Woodward

*Jacqueline H. Woodward lost her husband, Gary Alan Woodward, to COVID on November 28, 2020. He spent the last twenty-four days of life in the COVID critical care unit at Saint Thomas West Hospital in Nashville, being cared for by the same team he had led, and where he had worked as an RN for twenty-five years.*

Gary Alan Woodward, the love of my life, left this earth far too soon. Displaying a personality bigger than life, Gary poured his love onto his family every day. It is that love I carry on this new journey—a life that is filled with the memories of his distinct laughter, his strong comforting hands, and his service to others. As a critical care RN team leader, Gary gave his heart and soul to caring for those who were at a critical point, clinging to life.

How do I move forward without my spouse of forty-five years? I posture myself at the feet of my Lord and Savior, daily seeking His strength. It is there I'm reminded of all the ordinary things Gary and I experienced together: anxiously awaiting the birth of our three beautiful daughters; sitting on the front porch swing, enjoying the beauty of the landscape around us; family gatherings filled with laughter and love; holding hands as we walked side by side in the hardware store; playing a round of golf, enjoying our time on the course, under the blue sky; "glowing" together as we held each of our six grandchildren for the first time.

The joy of all the major family events, trips, and milestones are embedded in my heart. Gary made each of them a special time not only for me but for our three daughters as well. He made it obvious we were the center of his life. Retrieving those memories lessens the pain of my grief. It's amazing how tears of sadness can flow at the same time a bright smile appears on my face.

There are many days that I ask, "What would Gary do?" It is in those moments I feel closest to him. The exact words Gary would say begin to flow through my head. There are other times I replay his voicemails just to hear Gary say, "Hey Babe, I love you" or, "I didn't want anything, I was just calling to check on how your day is going." Gary always had the perfect timing to know when I needed him the most.

Gary Alan Woodward is gone from this earth. May he never be forgotten.

# THE OTHER THINGS
# I LEARNED FROM COVID

## Dr. Krishna Sankaran

*Dr. Krishna Sankaran is a nephrologist and professor. He lives and practices in Illinois.*

I never understood the mentality of soldiers—people willing to work on a job with the constant possibility of danger and death. But when the COVID epidemic first emerged, I started to understand. Most of my life, over thirty years, I've practiced medicine. Now, though, there was a new urgency and inherent risk because three in ten COVID patients need the care of a nephrologist, and I was one of the specialists equipped to help. Most of my colleagues in our practice have young children, but since mine are grown and I am at a different place in my life, I decided to be the one who would cover the cases in the hospital. In the early days of the pandemic, I worked eighty days in a row and was fortunate not to become ill. I cannot claim extreme courage or bravery, but I realized how, like a soldier, I was tasked to do my best, no matter the risk. I hold the ultimate respect for others who were not so fortunate, who died giving everything they had in service to their patients. And I hold the painful knowledge of the families left behind.

---

Helplessness is a profoundly disabling feeling. The medical community prides itself on its training in science and the practice of medicine with positive outcomes. Even when a prognosis is poor, we keep trying to help our patients, we keep trying not to fail. But with COVID, faced with an unknown pathogen and few guidelines for treatment, we were dealt failure after failure. During my career, I became used to seeing occasional death, but at no time in those years had I seen so many deaths every day, every week, for months on end. The helplessness was compounded by knowing I was one of the people best trained to help, yet I felt relatively useless. Coping was difficult. Every moment I could spare, I was studying the current knowledge—what they were doing in New York, what seemed to be helping—educating myself through my infectious disease peers, working to do the best I could. Years ago, as a young resident, I had worked in the first AIDS center in Chicago. I had already worn an orthopedic isolation suit, had already experienced the uncertainty of confronting the unknown. And now, it seemed to be happening again.

———————

As a physician, I have seen the effect of death on families, but COVID is different and brutal. So many patients die unexpectedly and rapidly, and for many months, their grief-stricken families couldn't stand by them, couldn't hold the dying one's hand to comfort them. This isolation was extremely painful. Even when a patient was on the point of death, we couldn't let loved ones in. Some patients had contact via FaceTime with their families, but these visits were harried and surreal. Things were so busy, and there were other desperately sick patients to connect via tablets and phones. And so most died with only compassionate staff to offer them solace. My own son was then in his first days as an ICU nurse. I witnessed his devastation over losing patients he had poured his soul into helping. I did the only thing I could for him—I listened, which was an intimate and humbling experience as a parent *and* as a physician.

One of my very first COVID patients was a man around my own age who died very fast. In those terrible early days, I had no time to get to know the man or his family but could only move on to the next very sick patient. A night later, the full echoes of the loss hit me. I was home, watching a news show that ended with a nightly tribute to a COVID victim who had died in the US. And there before me was my patient, but this time, he was alive, in a holiday photo, surrounded by his wife and four children—just as I was at that very moment, with my own wife, my own four children.

I thought about how when my kids were young, I hated traveling to conferences. I'd worry I would catch something and bring it home to them or that the plane would crash and my short absence would become permanent. What would they do without me? I hadn't thought about that untethered anxiety in years, but here it was again, visiting me. This was March 2020, a twisted beginning to the spring season. What would come next? What would they do without us?

# OUR HEALTH CARE HERO

## Pamela Addison

*Pamela Addison lost her husband, Martin Addison, to COVID on April 29, 2020.*

A hero is defined as a person who is admired and idealized for their courage and achievements, and my husband is the embodiment of this definition. He walked into his hospital every day at the start of this pandemic despite knowing the risks. As more and more COVID patients were being brought in, he still did his job as a speech pathologist the way he always did, with passion and dedication.

Unknowingly, he entered a room to assess a patient and, in doing so, caught COVID. A few days later, he felt his first symptom . . . just a cough, but because of the person, the hero he was, he did not report to work as instructed because he knew how many people he would come into contact with, and he loved his coworkers, who were like family, and he didn't want to put them at risk. Instead, he stayed home and isolated until he could get a test to affirm whether he had COVID, but soon one symptom turned into several. We didn't need the test to know COVID was in our house.

There are no certain words to describe losing your husband so suddenly and unexpectedly. I'd thought he was on the road to recovery. I was told tomorrow was going to be a better day, but two hours later, I saw the hospital number pop up on my phone, and I knew the news wasn't going to be good. However, nothing prepared me for the five words: "Martin went into cardiac arrest." Despite the physician assistant—who had become my friend and confidante in the twenty-six days Martin fought for his life in the hospital—telling me they were going to work on him, I knew the next call I would get from the hospital would announce Martin didn't make it. Thirty minutes later, I got that exact call. He'd bravely fought COVID for over a month, but the virus had done too much damage to his young and healthy body. My love, my hero, Elsie and Graeme's Papa, the person I was meant to grow old with, was gone.

How was I going to tell Elsie (only two) that Papa wasn't ever going to walk through our front door again? How was I going to make sure that Graeme (only five months) would know who Papa was? Martin's fear while he was isolating at home was that Graeme wouldn't remember him when he got better, but now he was gone, and I knew I had to make sure that Graeme would not only remember Martin but also get to know exactly who his Papa was.

In the years since Martin has passed, I have kept that promise, and now that the children are older, they have slowly started to grasp why Papa is no longer here with us. Elsie talks about him every single day. She mentions happy moments she remembers, asks to watch videos of her and Papa together, especially the one from her second birthday—she loves watching them make her special birthday unicorn birthday cake together. "Mommy, can we make the cake that I made with Papa again?" is what she usually asks after the video ends. Ironically, her last birthday with Martin was the day before he became ill. She also constantly looks at pictures and talks about them, like the one with him singing "Row, Row, Row Your Boat" with her and Graeme. She keeps the owl light on in her room at night because Papa was the one who always shut it off with her; she tells me that Papa is in heaven and always in her heart because she loves and misses him; and most recently, she questions me about his job and asks how he helped people in the hospital. I always make sure to tell her he is a hero, and she says one day, she wants to work in a hospital and be a hero too, just like him.

Graeme talks about how his Papa died and is in his heart. He carries Martin's keys around with him wherever he goes, he strums on the guitars Martin had bought him, and he loves going down to the basement to look at Papa's special guitars that he wants upstairs in his room. He intently watches "his man" across the street, who from behind is a spitting image of Martin, blow leaves and mow the lawn; he fills his backpack with things his Papa needs because Graeme still doesn't fully understand where Papa is—a someplace he cannot visit.

Martin is a part of Elsie and Graeme's every day, and when I hear them talking to each other about Papa or asking me questions about him, I know I have done what I needed to do. They know how much Papa loves and cares about them, and they want to know more about their hero. Elsie and Graeme need to know that others see him as the hero he truly is, and that is why I continue to share our story with the world—not only to honor Martin but to make sure their father, our health care hero, is never forgotten.

# THE LOST KEYS THAT FOUND ME

### Dawn Sizemore Adams

*Dawn Sizemore Adams is a nurse practitioner in Alabama. She lost her father, Tommy Sizemore, to COVID on January 5, 2021.*

August 21—my birthday: blue and purple balloons, my favorite yellow roses from my sweet husband and son, ice cream cake. And then it hit me as my husband said, "Make a wish."

Instantly, my heart sank, hands cold and clammy, a lump in my throat as if I was about to be sick, but from what? From the realization that it was the second birthday where I was aware my wish could never come true. Despite nearly three years of diagnosing COVID patients and enduring virus denial, despite mask backlash and vaccine refusal, despite all the vitriol, the ache of losing my father to COVID has only grown. Being a caregiver often means having to suppress your own backstory, but the backwash of COVID has changed how I cope, and no other experiences in my years of being a nurse practitioner are comparable.

There was an awkward silence after the birthday song as everyone stood still, staring at me. It's as if they were waiting for me to completely melt down. Even though on the inside I was a total wreck, I managed to hold back the tears, wishing my Pop was here to sing "Happy Birthday" and tease me about my age. My husband and son handed me my gift, creatively concealed in a deceptively oversized box. As I slowly opened the wrappings, I couldn't believe what I saw—they'd managed to find me the best birthday present I will ever receive—a set of plastic keys from the 1986 Fisher-Price My Pretty Purse set. Immediately, I began crying, and there was nothing I could do to stop. They knew how much those keys meant to me.

Pop owned his own appliance business and operated several coin-operated laundries across Alabama. During the summer, all I wanted to do was ride with him to the laundries and watch him pull the machines. When I was six years old, Pop bought me the My Pretty Purse set, and I carried it with me everywhere. I still vividly remember the golden yellow exterior with small pink flowers on the bottom right. Inside the purse came a play tube of lipstick, a light blue comb, and a set of two keys—one yellow, one red—attached to a key ring with an image of a little girl with blonde hair in pigtails, which Pop always told me was me. I loved that purse, especially the keys. It made me feel like a grown-up. When I would ride with Pop to the laundries, he always carried his ring of keys to pull the machines. So I carried my keys too and pretended I was pulling the machines with him. Those were the best days of my life.

One sunny summer day, Pop and I had gone to KFC to pick up Sunday dinner. I carried my purse in with me. When we returned home, I ran back to Pop's truck because I noticed I didn't have my purse. It was gone. I immediately burst into tears in our driveway. Pop got down on his knees and hugged me. I still remember leaning into his chest, crying, the smell of his cologne, his soft, reassuring voice. We went back to KFC later, but my purse wasn't there. Suddenly, I learned what the word "stolen" meant and how it made me feel. Pop must have bought me a million other purses to try and replicate my Pretty

Purse. But none would ever bring me the same joy as holding that plastic purse with those keys in it, pretending to pull the machines and get the coins out with my Dad.

When Pop died, I felt like a little girl lost in a grocery store. A little girl who was holding her dad's hand but who somehow got accidentally separated. A feeling of sheer panic and fear set in. I felt permanently lost until that magic moment when I saw my keys in a huge box. I was no longer lost, though who would have ever dreamed that all it would take to find me was a simple set of red and yellow plastic keys? Thank you, Pop, for giving me a lifetime of beautiful memories to hold in my heart forever. As for my keys, I still carry them with me everywhere.

# WRITING IT ALL DOWN

Laura Jesmer

*Laura Jesmer is an LCSW therapist who lives in Arizona. She lost her mother, Frances Kapp, to COVID on November 27, 2020.*

As a psychotherapist in practice for the past thirty years, I have worked with hundreds of people who have experienced traumatic events, including health challenges, periods of extreme stress and distress, and the loss of loved ones. Grief and trauma are part of the human experience, one that most of us have had and will experience again. Several therapeutic modalities have proven to be effective in trauma treatment and the journey of loss, mourning, and grief. Writing is one form of therapeutic and creative expression that has been beneficial to many. Through writing in an intimate way, we can literally feel the emotions that we may want to convey, even to others who we otherwise would never connect with.

I have been working with clients during the pandemic whose loved ones have died of COVID, but I also lost my mother to the virus in November of 2020. Research certainly substantiates the benefits of writing on grief journeys, and my personal experience also supports this assertion. Writing it down brings the emotional pain of loss into the physical world. The written word is illuminating and is proof that it happened. That's why writing can be so healing—it brings the hidden wound into the open; now you can see it, point to it—this is what happened—and putting it into words, I can give it the care and attention it needs.

In a recent interview by Minnie Driver on her podcast, *Minnie Questions*, writer Anthony Doerr described the enormity of writing about the details of a person's life because it connects human beings across time and space. He suggests that writing is an act of "imaginative empathy," sharing about the uniqueness of a person while also allowing the reader to feel the similarities inherent in humanity. I believe it helps us feel less alone while honoring the lives of those we lost. Sometimes I write about fond memories because sensory experience is my rich entryway into the past, whether I share what I write or not, and when I remember my mother, my memories sustain me in ways that COVID stole and that others have minimized.

I think of her laugh, the image of her standing in front of a beautiful flower, of her lighting the Shabbat candles and eating challah at Friday night dinners, and often, baseball. Mom grew up with the love of the game, but initially, it was for the Chicago White Sox. Her father loved baseball and always rooted for the Sox. They lived on the southwest side of the city, so that was their team. Mom's parents owned a small grocery in the forties and early fifties, where she and her younger sister spent time with their parents listening to and watching White Sox games. The love of baseball was intimately intertwined with their love for one another.

Later, after my Mom's father had died, my grandmother took a job on the North Side of Chicago and moved the family closer to work. While she would always remain a White Sox fan, Mom was now surrounded by Cubs fans and became a die-hard fan herself. She had more than enough love in her heart for both teams, and this adoration persisted and was handed down to my brother and I, especially in our attachment to the Cubs. We will always treasure the times we were able to share with my Mom, attending games and watching them at home together, talking about pitchers over a meal, and sharing a joyous midnight phone call in November 2016 after the Cubs miraculously won the World Series.

I will always treasure the memory of my Mom making her regular spring training visit, as she did every year since I moved to Phoenix in the mid-nineties. To get to see her Cubbies in the sunny Arizona spring, especially while it was cold, dreary, and gray in Chicago, gave a glimmer of hope that winter would thaw and the most wonderful season, baseball season, was arriving.

One year, my brother decided to surprise Mom by coming out to Arizona during his spring break from school. I took Mom out for lunch. David flew into Phoenix and took a cab to the restaurant. Sitting on the sunny patio, she had ordered her coffee, black, and was perusing the menu choices when David nonchalantly walked up to the table and said, "Hi, Mom!" It took a moment to register, her eyes widened, and then she exuberantly exclaimed, "David!!!" She was so happy to see him, loved that we surprised her, and, of course, we were excited to feel such joy.

Grief is intricate and full of nuance, so although we might need to recall an exuberant Cubs game, sometimes we also need to write about the pain. To be with the parts of us who have carried it all alone for all this time. Although it is difficult to discuss, I will share that I fantasized about ways to hide in the corner of my mother's hospital room, behind the reclining chair meant for a family member staying with their loved one before COVID times. Could I somehow make myself invisible so the nurses and doctors wouldn't find me when they told us it was time to leave? The thirty-minute rule due to possible deadly transmission of the virus be damned. I wanted to hold her hand all night and help her feel she was not alone. Maybe a part of me didn't care if I caught it, because being with her in her time of need was more important than the logical part of me that knew I couldn't stay. To leave the room, not knowing, but kind of knowing it would be the last time, was too much to bear. Two years later, I can let it out a little bit at a time. I have carried it around, and now, it slowly emerges through the pain in my body, in my heart, and onto the pages where I write it all down.

# Kindred
# Spirits

# PEOPLE ARE CRAZY

Every Friday night, after a long week at our body shop, we would head out for dinner and karaoke at a hole-in-the wall bar and grill. My husband and I would meet with our closest friends for a night of fun.

My husband's go-to song was always the same: "People are Crazy" by Billy Currington. The karaoke guy would announce us as "George and Company." We would all sing along with him—it was so much fun. Now that is my favorite song, and it brings back so many good memories. . .

I can see him, standing there with his cowboy hat and his long white beard, drinking his Coors Light and singing while everyone cheered him on.

I miss him every day.

—Mina Aguilera

# THE WORLD WAS ALSO WAITING TO GRIEVE

Rima Samman

*Rima Samman lost her brother, Rami Samman, to COVID on May 10, 2020.*

We were thirteen months apart. I only knew a year of life before he was born, but I have no recollection of it. My earliest memories all involve him. My future plans and goals involved him. I'd never thought of life without Rami. I was the older one, but people often thought we were twins. We had this bond where we knew we were there for each other, and more importantly, we knew we loved each other. Rami was amazing—no matter what our circumstances were (there had been times our family struggled), Rami could find ways to make the best of things.

When he passed away, I didn't understand. How could I lose my baby brother? This isn't the order of the way things go. His pale lifeless body on a gurney, my mother cradling him as she cried out, "My baby, my baby" over and over again. Why? What happened? It was the last time I'd see him. The last memory.

We could not hold a funeral because it was the peak of the pandemic, but I spent the next months writing to senators, attempting to begin investigations into Rami's death. I also walked the Belmar beach daily, finding solace in the ocean, picking up shells. Soon, Rami's forty-first birthday was approaching. I needed to do something, as I'd never known a time where we hadn't said "happy birthday" to each other. Death could not stop me. He might not have been here anymore, but I knew he was watching. I also needed to bring my mom a form of peace, as a part of her had died with him.

I decided I was going to make a yellow heart on the sand, composed of the clam shells I'd been collecting, surrounding it with enough candles that my brother could see it from heaven.

At first, I thought of writing on the shells, but my mom suggested placing a pebble inside the heart with his name. I liked the idea, but in order to fill the heart, we needed more than one pebble. I went on social media and announced I'd be lighting the heart on my brother's birthday, and I invited others to come add their loved ones' names. That night, about twenty-five people showed, and approximately 120 names were placed. My partner, Travis, helped me light more than two hundred candles. A mom and her daughter said a prayer, and John Walsh sang "Danny Boy." Unknown to him, it was my grandmother's favorite song.

My mom cried. She cried in a good way, the way we cry at a funeral, the way we cry when we're grieving and need to release our sadness, the way we cry when love overwhelms us. Travis and I cried as well. We walked away that night thinking we'd be back the next day to clean it up. I went to bed peaceful that evening for the first time in a long time. I had given my mom a space to say goodbye. I gave her a place to grieve. Little did I know the world was also waiting, just like us, for a place to grieve and gather with strangers who understood.

The next morning, images of the lit heart began to go viral. Little by little and day by day, the heart became twelve hearts bearing over 3,500 names. How could we stop when we knew the need for this space?

That's how it all began . . . and now, what was once clamshells and rocks on a beach has become the first permanent national COVID-19 memorial. It is known as Rami's Heart. People tell me I'm a hero, but I'm not. I'm just a sister who loves her brother beyond measure, and I won't allow his death to take that away. No matter how horrible it was, the world will know of him.

# BE NOT FOND OF FAIR WORDS

MARK ALDRICH

*Mark Aldrich lost his father, William Robert Aldrich, to COVID on May 10, 2020.*

I have started to cry in my dreams. This is a new development in my psychological history and not an unwelcome one, as I have not cried while awake in quite a long time. It means I want to cry. I get choked up quite easily, but then it doesn't happen. The cry.

This is not to say that I have started to cry in my sleep; no, I do not wake with a dampened face. In the last two and a half years, I have started to dream dreams in which I am in tears, really letting loose. At least once in a dream, I found myself on my hands and knees and watched the tears leave my eyes and puddle the ground, like a cartoon version of a healthy cry. My father walks past, sometimes just one more figure who strides by my crying self on the sidewalk in my hometown, sometimes someone who stops—always my father. He is genial. I am always aware that he is dead.

———————

My father died of COVID-19 on May 10, 2020, in the early months of the pandemic, less than forty-eight hours after he first tested positive. William Robert (Bob to all who met him) Aldrich was eighty-four.

I said to a friend two months earlier that I doubted I would personally know a victim or a person who came down with COVID. There are many occasions in which I need to be corrected, but this was the darkest. In the first weeks after his death, I wrote and published a few essays about my emotions and found myself in some unproductive online fights with pandemic deniers. My sister and I both spoke about our father's life with a *Boston Globe* journalist who had read one of my essays and who manned the COVID obituaries desk there. In practical terms, my sister accomplished more: she told our family's story of COVID loss to the local newspaper and landed my father's name on its front page. It was important to make clear to the world and to our neighbors that even though our father was eighty-four and had Alzheimer's disease, he did not die of anything other than COVID. This distinction is important as he could still be alive today. It is important because there are those who still deny COVID's devastating importance. When they meet my sister, mother, or me, they meet someone who suffered a COVID loss; they meet COVID's reality.

A year after my father's death, I was at my first social event, a large barbecue on a sunny Memorial Day at a park beside the Hudson River. Many of us had not seen each other in person for more than a year, and we were all newly vaccinated. Thus, the pandemic was the only topic of conversation, even if it was not what any group chatted about. An acquaintance that I had not seen in a few years started to discuss the pandemic with me in "big picture" terms. I do not think she knew of my personal loss. A woman who advocates for "mindfulness" and of living in the powerful "now," she spoke to me with clear-eyed intensity about how, "Maybe the planet needs a cleansing, maybe it is saying to us that there are too many of you."

My father's face floated up at me. The planet didn't need to be cleansed of him, I thought to myself. Because I have a pointless inner commitment to not create waves, though, I simply said, "Maybe" and excused myself to find a new conversation, which happened to be with someone to my immediate right. I did not identify myself to my acquaintance as someone whose own father had perished in the early portion of the pandemic. I wish I had. It may have helped her refine her thoughts to add some practical humanism to her spiritual revolution.

———————

I turned to literature in the months after my father's death. Poetry and music, not novels. In that first year of grief, a novel can seem like a description of someone else's dreams, a curious bit of writing that is not specifically applicable to one's own situation, which for me led to a self-centered desire to be understood rather than to understand.

Essays, also. I consumed Roland Barthes's *Mourning Diary*, composed by him for a year after his mother's death but unpublished until after his own. Handwritten on dated scraps of paper instead of in a book—so that he could capture the immediacy of his emotions in a rejection of any formal process like opening a book to the next available page and allowing his thoughts to coalesce before setting pen to paper—the diary mirrored my own emotional cloudiness while it also helped to clarify my thoughts to myself.

Early in his year of grief, Barthes writes, "How strange her voice, which I knew so well, and which is said to be the very texture of memory, I no longer hear. Like a localized deafness . . ." For many years, I had said that if my phone rang and one of my departed grandparents started to speak, I would recognize any of their voices even though I haven't heard any of them speak in decades. Now my father's voice had been added to that list, and here one of my intellectual heroes gave voice to a very similar thought-emotion. Death is a "localized deafness," a very specific sort of hearing loss, as if the voice is still available to be heard but blocked by the tinnitus of death.

The poetic nature of the line resonated with me as you can see (if not hear). I ran into a friend whose father had died at around the same time as mine, though not of COVID. I had recently read the above quote, so I shared it with her, with caveats offered that if she did not want to talk about our mutual losses, we could skip to anything else, like celebrity gossip. I read it to her. "I can still hear my father's voice," she protested, and she started to weep. I wished she had simply said, "Maybe" to me and turned to converse with someone else, but to her credit, we stayed with the moment. We appreciated each other's empathy. Perhaps Barthes's comment was too poetic, too far from her truth while so close to mine, or too close to her experience of grief for her to express with anything other than a rejection and tears. Grief is a localized hearing.

---

In my experience of this loss, I found that the fact of the loss ("my father died of COVID") supplanted the object of that sentence, my father himself. Who he was. It is understandable: something in me wanted to protect me from my own sharp emotion, my sense of loss. I searched for answers for my feelings before I had allowed myself to feel those feelings. I wanted answers before I knew how to phrase the questions.

Thus, Robert Burton's *The Anatomy of Melancholy*, a book-length essay on how to diagnose and cure melancholy, was a perfect volume for that desire. It is nothing but answers. First published in 1621, it is also approximately the same number of pages. "Melancholy" for Burton is an umbrella term that covers the vast range of human emotions, from irritation to mood changes to depression to madness, and, given the book's era, almost none of his medical advice, especially the bits about bloodletting to balance humors, is now practical. He suffered from obsessiveness, and we are all the richer for his compulsion to catalog every instance of "melancholy" he could find in his library in an effort to make sense of his own experience of his own emotions.

Every once in a while, I met my father in there. In Part II, "The Cure of Melancholy," Section 3, Member VII, "Against Repulse, Abuses, Injuries, Contempts, Disgraces, Contumelies, Slanders, Scoffs, etc." (as I said, he is a tad obsessive), Burton offers fourteen pages of injured reputations through ancient history and the Bible, retells some anecdotes, and then breaks down and states that there are so many "grievances which happen to mortals in this life" that what truly works are all the old sayings, and he presents two pages of homely admonitions that one might find written in needlepoint on a throw pillow: "Be not idle. Look before you leap." Stuff like that.

In this chapter about how to overcome the injuries of scoffs and scorn, Burton suggests the entire collection of corny precepts (some of them were corny already in his own time): "If thou seest aught amiss in another, mend it in thyself. . . . Find no faults, meddle not with another man's matters. . . . Be not unthankful. Be meek, merciful, and patient. Do good to all. Be not fond of fair words."

And there was my dad. Not my "father who died of COVID." My dad, who was not "fond of fair words." He was not a quotable phrase-turner, except for his occasional spoonerisms, but he is in those corny bits of advice, is visible even in the corniness itself.

One day when I was in my teens, I confided to him that I had feelings for someone, and he said the one thing that I still quote from my unquotable dad: "It's never wrong to say, 'I love you.'" Decades later, I've learned through my further adventures in like-lust-love that this advice is thoroughly true and never wrong.

It is as good advice as any found in *The Anatomy of Melancholy*. Two and a half years into the pandemic, the death of my father is a fact about which I am angry, is a loss that inspires a passion that all of us who have lost loved ones find recognition and a public solace in, but perhaps I used the fervor of both of these thoughts to not acknowledge the pain of the loss of my dad inside the "death of my father from COVID."

Absent the public activity and petitions and passion for justice in the face of a crisis that struck the heart of my family, absent the agitations, we can find simple, plain grief, which is always a form of gratitude that love exists. The simple is always healthier; Robert Burton and my dad would agree on this. There is no right way to mourn or wrong way to grieve. It's never wrong to say, "I love you."

# OFTEN OUR BANGING BECAME MUSIC

BOB GREENBERG

*Bob Greenberg lost two friends, Olan Montgomery and Ian Finkel, to COVID. Olan died on April 4, 2020. Ian died on November 16, 2020.*

In 2020, at the start of the lockdown in New York City, people took to applauding our essential workers at 7:00 p.m. People played their trumpets or hit pots and pans or just clapped outside their windows or on balconies. We'd all seen similar images coming first from Italy—people singing to each other across the air, but the alleys below were empty. And now we were doing this in New York, where the crawls at the bottom of our TV screens were dire amidst images of refrigerated trucks parked outside hospitals.

I live at Manhattan Plaza at Forty-Third Street, which is two high buildings, one on Ninth Avenue and the other on Tenth with a plaza in between. Our residents are mostly actors, musicians, playwrights, and seniors. As the pandemic took hold, our buildings took part in the ritual. It was comforting to "connect" with my neighbors, many of whom I didn't know despite decades of living there, from 7:00 to 7:15 p.m. every night.

Often our banging became music . . .

As time passed, fewer and fewer people continued the 7:00 p.m. ritual, but I noticed that there were still people doing it outside—not just from windows, out on our plaza. I decided to go down and join the group. We kept our distance, wore our masks, and banged away outside come rain or shine.

Sometimes it was freezing and snowing, but still we showed up. We called ourselves "The Social Distancenaires" and "We Clap Because We Care." We soon started to get to know each other and even began to party a bit afterward, celebrating each other's birthdays and other milestones. Most importantly, we got to know each other and keep tabs on one another.

Three years later, and we are the last remaining people clapping for essential and frontline workers in New York. But we persist; we even shake tambourines. Now that there is an alleged return to normal, it's often hard for all of us to be there every night, yet there's somehow always a minyan, or close to one! We bang and chant and sing and shout, "Thank you!"

Why we're still clapping together is hard to say. We all have our own reasons. For me, it's about honoring and remembering. Early in the pandemic, I lost two friends to COVID, and another is still with us but was terribly compromised, so like many New Yorkers, this is personal for me. Our city is not the same; there are winds of grief blowing if you stop and listen—and you should.

One of my friends who died, Olan, was an actor who was similar to me in type so we often saw each other at auditions. There was never any rivalry between us. In fact, at the end of our last audition, just as the virus was beginning, he gave me a hug and a kiss goodbye on the cheek. At the time, it struck me as odd but heartwarming, as he hadn't ever done that before. I never saw him again.

I think about that moment a lot. I replay it, often when I'm clapping for the people who I hope may have helped my friends. We are so thankful to all those who never stopped working and sacrificed their own safety during the pandemic, whether they're doctors or nurses or they work in food delivery or maintenance. I wonder where we would all be without them. I think about Olan's hug. I kiss him goodbye on the cheek.

# NO SLEEP TILL BROOKLYN

Lisa Smid

*Lisa Smid lost her boyfriend, Ben Schaeffer, and her friend, Emily Rosenberg, to COVID. Ben died on April 28, 2020. Emily died on January 12, 2021.*

## I. Been

He'd been a rabble-rouser from the start. From our second date on, Ben stashed stories of his past and present in one of those wrinkled, oval-handed, black plastic bags you carry out of New York bodegas. When we dined at "the pizza store," these bags of tricks held Ben's daily show-and-tell objects. Photos from day trips to Albany. Spoof postcards from his union mocking the transit authority CEO. Random news clippings. Ben bagged every abandoned newspaper on his subway train at the end of each day's shift to read later. But some items were about him. Letters to the editor. A photo of Ben counter-protesting the Westboro Baptist Church at a Brooklyn synagogue. And then, the story of his fight with the Metropolitan Transit Authority to create a subway conductor's yarmulke.

Rumbles with the MTA had never been anything new. A shop steward and eventual vice chair of his transit union, and a community activist on his own time, he'd been fighting for other people's rights. His own rights were no exception.

An Orthodox Jew, Ben always covered his head. On the subway, he alternated between the round conductor's cap in spring and fall and the plush blue winter ushanka with the conductor badge embedded into the fuzz. But he was not to wear the black yarmulke he tucked neatly under his off-duty baseball cap. Anything a transit employee wore must be part of the uniform. New York summers make a subway conductor's booth too hot for more than a light skullcap. A Sikh coworker had successfully fought the transit authority for the right to wear a turban. In time, a turban with the standard MTA logo was available for this man to order. So in what Ben described to me later as "the Ben Schaeffer way of doing things," he started his own head-covering dialogue by ordering a turban for himself.

"You're not getting a turban," Ben quoted the higher-ups' reply.

While Ben went through his union for backup, he also consulted a *posek*, a scholar who determines the position of Jewish law in cases where previous authorities are inconclusive. The first rabbi he consulted said it was okay to go bareheaded under the circumstances. Unsatisfied, Ben moved on to the headquarters at Agudath Israel, where the rabbis not only provided documentation on the religious requirement to cover his head but also profiled Ben in their newsletter. Soon, a yarmulke with the MTA insignia was created. All Ben had to do was order it like any part of his uniform.

On one date, fortified with lunch from the pizza store and the triumphant yarmulke tale, I accompanied Ben to work on his subway train. Before showing me the works in the conductor's booth, he had to clock in. I excitedly waited outside the MTA employee lounge at Coney Island-Stillwell Avenue to check out this aforementioned bespoke yarmulke firsthand.

When Ben emerged from the lounge, his far-receded hairline was bare, bereft even of the usual black yarmulke.

The spot was large enough for me to press my hand against it without touching any hair. (Since he was a head taller and I had to stand shoeless on the couch to be eye-level with him, the palm-on-the-bald-spot anchor would prove useful while hugging or kissing him.) Fair-skinned Ben was "Lobster Boy at the Beach," so his scalp probably benefited from coverage this skullcap provided on days like that August Sunday.

"Where's the MTA yarmulke?" I demanded.

"I never ordered it," he told me. Tension and hostility rise during service delays. Wearing anything identifying himself as Jewish made him a target at certain stops on his train.

"So what was the whole point of fighting for the yarmulke?"

"I wasn't going to let them tell me I couldn't wear it."

Years into our relationship, I'd ask him to order the MTA yarmulke for me . . . to no avail.

The MTA's "not part of the uniform" pretext was one excuse for forbidding transit workers to wear masks in the early days of the pandemic. Was there no time to fight? Ben is one of 173 transit workers who didn't make it back to work.

## II. For Emily, Whenever I May Find Her

"No, no, I want to hear *all* about you first," Emily's Twitter bio proclaims.

She was as good a listener as she was a reader. Sunday mornings were at Brooklyn's Tea Lounge, our table illuminated more by the white apples of surrounding Mac laptops than by any sunlight or lamp fixtures. Over full wooden trays of loose tea and cruets of honey, we'd chew the cud on the news, our workshop that week, and our boyfriends, Emily nodding with her large, sympathetic brown eyes, before we turned to our laptops and hammered out bits and pieces of fiction. When

I'd head out into the light toward Prospect Park, Emily was still writing.

We'd frequented the same women writer's workshop. Women came and went, drifted away like unfinished sentences. But Emily was a constant those Wednesday nights at 7:00. The quietest among us, she'd come to life with the instigation of more gregarious company. When Ben picked me up for a date after one workshop and engaged Emily in Brooklyn politics, she rose to the occasion like a freshly watered flower.

When I left town indefinitely, we kept up the Wednesday nights at 7:00 p.m.—Brooklyn time. We migrated from Skype to FaceTime to Facebook Messenger . . . me firing off meaty paragraphs, her replying in short, succinct sticks of sentences. Emily crafted delightfully snappy episode recaps for a reality show blog. She sold jokes and shared some on her Twitter feed.

"I want to hug a lion," she tweeted. "Can someone hook me up?"

"I'd be 'lion' if I said I could," I offered back.

Those Messenger paragraph clouds of mine mushroomed. When my mother died and I cleaned out her home. When the estate was settled and I returned to New York to reunite with Ben. When my father fell and needed rehab, necessitating a return to Nashville. When COVID made its way around weeks later and my still-recovering dad insisted on shopping maskless during the lockdown. When Ben was on the ventilator with the virus, fighting for his life, and I desperately tried to get him convalescent plasma. When he was buried in a faraway place. When I myself got exposed to COVID. Emily always listened. I really tried to give her equal time, hear her thoughts, even in my anguish. She texted about being tired, with doctors adjusting her thyroid meds. She only went out to the store and doctor's appointments.

Before Thanksgiving 2020, things went silent. I left anxious voicemails. December 3, Emily groggily called back to say she was in the hospital after falling. She was undergoing tests. "So, consider yourself assured," she said.

"Emily is not currently capable of making or receiving phone calls," her boyfriend emailed me weeks later. "At present she is in the ICU because of breathing difficulties; last time I saw her, she was asleep, with an oxygen tube down her throat. . . . Prior to going to the ICU, she was only intermittently awake and sentient. She just went for another MRI yesterday in order to determine whether a biopsy on the more serious of her brain lesions is even possible."

Before the biopsy results, Emily went into cardiac arrest in the respiratory unit. She was gone.

It wasn't until family friends tagged Emily in Facebook posts that I learned the whole truth. "COVID complications from brain tumor issues"; "Secondary infection . . ."

I knew she'd been hospitalized for weeks. What I didn't understand was how a dear friend could die of a virus in the hospital that she didn't have when she entered.

Zoom showed an open grave ready to receive Emily. No view of the casket, just resounding thuds of dirt. From the waist up, I suited up with the black Hermès plissé scarf I'd planned to show her.

I haven't replayed the recorded Zoom shiva that followed days later. If I do, the more I'll lose of Emily bit by bit. Or rather, I'll misplace her and not be able to find her again.

If I sit somewhere and listen closely, keep my eyes out, Emily will come back into view. Ben will ask her about the Brooklyn City Council races, I'll show her my new scarf, we will all relax and settle into our element, we will all slowly and delightedly rise to life.

# THE THINGS I CAN'T FIX

## Catherine Sasanov

*Catherine Sasanov lost several close friends and family members to COVID.*

Under another name, I work as a personal organizer. I pride myself on being the one who calmly walks into chaos and talks clients down off their cliffs (though, as I stress to those clients, I am not a therapist or priest; there are problems I'm not qualified to solve, sins I'm not in the position to forgive. And yet, like therapists and priests, I do take the vow of silence). Objects and papers that paralyze others have no power over me. That said, I respect people's possessions. I don't force anyone to throw things away. I'm often the one person a client has in their life who they know will not judge them, who they feel they can trust with their secrets if secrets must be revealed in order for me to work most effectively. At times, I've kept folks from losing their jobs, their homes, their marriages, their minds. I helped suicide-proof a condo once so a small child couldn't lose her life. I've had to learn that, with some jobs, no matter how hard I work, it will never be enough. A woman once hired me to declutter her small, three-room apartment (a space surreally housed in a run-down, carved-up, late eighteenth-century mansion turned rooming house). As I began to work, she revealed to me how her only child, a policewoman, had been recently murdered, shot by a boyfriend using the officer's own service revolver. The grief was gutting the mother and leaving her living space in chaos. As

I moved through the place, trying to silence the visual noise, bring some semblance of order back to her home, every piece of furniture I touched seemed to fall apart. Legs would fall off, tables would buckle, collapse. I'd gently prop them back up, move on. It was as if the furnishings themselves couldn't bear the grief.

———————

Within a month of COVID entering Boston, I went from being the guy on the white horse riding in to save folks from clutter to possibly the angel of death. Within a month, none of my clients wanted to get near me. And I didn't want to get near them. Already, I was watching what death could do, walking into the homes of people I knew under the guise of "help": in March, my sister-in-law lost her mother in New York after the woman who cared for her brought COVID into the home; in Illinois, my beloved college literature teacher (whose Oklahoma drawl I can still hear in my head, reciting from heart his favorite poems) died after a wellness visit by his physical therapist. The hospital staff snuck his wife into the ICU to see him at the end. She gave the nurse attending her dying, intubated husband the stack of poems she and her husband loved to read to each other. Pressing herself against the glass, she could hear the nurse reading those poems to her husband until he finally drew his last breath. Those first horrible months, the deaths were unrelenting: the shopkeeper we'd always see when we made our yearly vacation to Maine, recovering nicely in the hospital from routine surgery, caught COVID and died within days; a good friend lost his only sibling, his longest and dearest friend. In early 2020, she'd accepted her current doctor's offer to remedy a bungled surgery from years before. While recovering in rehab, she began to sicken. In her brother's eighty-five years on earth, no matter how far he and his sister might be from one another, a day never went by when they didn't talk. He told me how, as the sick days passed, their phone conversations grew shorter, her voice got weaker and weaker, until their talks were him just listening to her breathe. Death finally snuffed out even that small connection. By the end of 2021, six people I knew had died of COVID, leaving a world of grief in their wake. Yet most of my friends, most of my clients, didn't know anyone who'd died. Some didn't even know someone who'd been sick.

---

The long arms of COVID nearly destroyed my business, like so many others. During the long hiatus in our work, some of my clients died, and many moved away. Others changed work hours and availability. Some took the skills I'd modeled over the years and learned to apply them themselves. Much of my work now is packing folks up: for a move across town, to a new town, to another state. Vaccinated, ventilated, we again work together side by side. But not everyone. I worry about the conservative client who won't get vaccinated for political reasons, the liberal client who won't vaccinate her child for fear the girl might lose her future fertility. I want to tell them how it felt to empty the apartment of a woman who shouldn't be dead. Standing alone in her apartment, trash bag in hand, I wasn't sure who I was angrier at: the surgeon who, decades earlier, had destroyed much of the woman's sight during a botched procedure, or the current purveyors of misinformation who'd convinced her getting vaccinated would rob her of the last of her sight. I want to tell my unvaccinated clients how it felt to sit on the couch off of which EMTs lifted her body too late to save her; how ugly it felt to be handling her things without her permission. The despair I felt at one point, looking at a bottle cap set aside in a drawer; my inability to divine whether it was trash or treasure, a portal, perhaps, into the happiest of memories or a touchstone to a long-lost love. I worry about the client who, in spite of taking every precaution for the past two years, ended up infected. I'm concerned about the brain fog she can't seem to shake, the unspoken fear it puts in both of us since her family has a history of dementia. Having lost my father to the illness, I want to save her that fate. But that need is beyond my skills. I can declutter a home, but I can't relieve the pain of the client who cried out once in the middle of our work, "I am so lonely," pulled herself together, and went on as if nothing had occurred. At the end of our session, at the end of every session, with every client, I'm paid, and we part until I'm called in again. I love my clients, and it grieves me that there will always be things I can't fix in their lives. COVID has only made that truth more profound.

# LAUGHTER WAS AT THE CENTER OF OUR RELATIONSHIP

### DIANE HAWKINS

*Diane Hawkins lost her aunt, Joyce Bugg, to COVID on January 28, 2021.*

I went most of my life without talking to my Aunt Joyce Bugg only because we lived in different cities, but when she moved to Radcliff, Kentucky, eighteen years ago, I made sure to be around her on a regular basis. My mother always wanted me to get to know her sister, and this was my opportunity. We talked and laughed—on the phone, at the movies, and over countless lunches and dinners with a huge side of laughter. She even met my friends, making them her friends with her unique sense of humor.

I was her "faaaaavorite niece," but I reminded her that I was her "only niece."

"That's not the point!"

Several years ago, I was leaving her house in Radcliff, and a wayward deer appeared to be charging toward us but ran farther away. "Rudolph" was more afraid of us than anything, but we still bumped into each other trying to get back into the house.

"I saved your life!" she said proudly.

Her so-called heroic effort made her feel good—that's all that mattered.

Another time, I was visiting my aunt in the hospital, and she needed a blood transfusion. The nurse walked into her room and announced, "I have your B-positive ready." I perked up and said, "Hey, that's my blood type, too. So, it's in our blood to 'be positive,' get it?"

"Get out!" she said, feigning disapproval of my clever pun. Actually, she thought it was funny that I stayed in her room, laughing at my own joke.

During the pandemic, we resorted to talking on the phone. When I did come to visit, it was only to knock on her door and drop off food supplies and face masks, including one designed with Michelle Obama's image, which she loved. For social distancing purposes, I would leave before she could open the door.

Several months later, there was one time I couldn't reach her on the phone. Knowing that I would be worried, her son called to tell me that my aunt had been rushed to the hospital with COVID-19. Thank God the hospital's nurses allowed us to talk to her on FaceTime. My aunt always had a sense of humor, even throughout her hospital stays with heart issues. This last time was not any different, and she joked with my cousins and me without missing a beat.

Even though the nurses warned us that she didn't have long to live, my aunt's personality was still as strong as ever. Maybe the nurses were incorrect.

Unfortunately, they weren't wrong, and I have missed my aunt every day since January 28, 2021. There are times when I look in the mirror and I'm reminded of her because of my dimples—a family trait.

I guess I'm meant to smile so that I can see them. I like to think that's another reason why she always tried to make me laugh.

# TIARA AND SASH

Rosie Davis

*Rosie Davis lost her mother, Mary Castro, to COVID, on May 17, 2020.*

My mom was everything—she was a mom, dad, grandmother, and great-grandmother. She was a fashionista who wore all the latest trends and always looked her best. She loved getting dolled up for special occasions and always looked forward to having her hair and makeup done. Her birthday was a very special day, and she made sure everyone knew it. There was always a long process to prepare for her big day. She had to have the perfect outfit, accessories, nails, hair, and makeup. There was a mental checklist. My mom had a birthday wish list ready for all of us so we could each pick an item to buy. Her presents had to be wrapped, and the cake had to be decorated in her favorite pink—her signature color. The most important piece to her big day, other than family, was her tiara and sash. She was the matriarch of our family, royalty if you will. There was no birthday if there was no tiara and sash.

I loved watching her on her big day. She was so excited about every little detail that went into her celebration. The brand-new clothes, jewelry, cake, and presents all for her, she was the center of attention, and she knew how loved she was.

In March 2020, nursing homes in the Dallas area went into lockdown. I was so scared as I watched residents in nursing homes across the country dying from this new virus called COVID-19. No one knew what this monster was; all we knew was it was taking lives very quickly. My fear for my mom grew as the case numbers kept climbing in the Dallas area. My mom had early-onset dementia; she didn't understand what had just happened. All she knew was that her daughter was no longer allowed to visit her in person. My mom was stripped away from me long before she died.

April 9, 2020, my mom's last birthday: I knew I had to try to make her special day as special as possible. I had several phone calls with her leading up to her birthday, and every one ended with her asking if we would spend her day together. It broke my heart. For the first time in my life, I would not be spending her birthday with her. There would be no shopping for the perfect outfit or doing her makeup, nails, and hair. She didn't understand why we couldn't be there. She thought I was mad at her and didn't want to be with her. My family and I made beautiful fruit trays and baked dozens of cupcakes to take to the nursing home. I delivered everything, including her tiara and sash. I begged the staff to take pictures and video of them singing "Happy Birthday." The big window in the lobby is what kept me from hugging and kissing my mom. I put my hand on the window, and she put hers on the glass too, and I looked at her and said, "Happy birthday, Mom. I love you and I'm sorry I can't be with you."

I felt robbed, and I'm sure she felt the same. When I got home, I broke down and waited impatiently for pictures and the video. I finally received them. I could tell she was trying to make the best of her day, but how could she when she had to spend it with strangers? I watched the video of everyone singing "Happy Birthday." She had a little smile on her face with her tiara and sash on and she was the center of attention. My mom turned seventy-five that day, not knowing it would be her last birthday.

Mother's Day 2020: the last day I would see my mother's face. She was so weak; the virus had found my mom. She was already isolated from everyone except the health care workers in the nursing home because she was one of the most vulnerable, and there was no protection. My mom was taken to a hospital two days later, and she fought for five days before she lost her battle to this monster called COVID-19. I made it my mission to humanize the number that once drowned out my mom as a person. I started the Yellow Heart Memorial to honor every life lost to COVID. I created a space and a way for communities to come together to grieve.

Twice, I have walked across the Brooklyn Bridge with hundreds of other members of the COVID survivor community, from many organizations, walking in solidarity with Yellow Heart. I do this in honor of the woman who gave me life—my mentor, my hero—and I did it wearing a tiara and sash. She will forever be our matriarch, and she is now known worldwide as Mary Castro.

# TO INFINITY AND BEYOND

MARY MANTELL AND ALEXANDRIA MANTELL

*Mary Mantell lost her husband, and Alexandria Mantell lost her father, Mike Mantell, to COVID on April 14, 2020.*

## I. Continuum, Friendship

COVID has taken so much from so many people. If you weren't affected by it, then you want it all to be over and to live your normal life, but for millions, the trauma and grief will never be over.

There is one positive thing COVID has done, though— it's brought those of us who have lost someone together and allowed us to form inseparable bonds. Over Zoom calls and in online support sessions, I have met wonderful, caring people who understand my loss. They get what it feels like to take your loved one to a hospital and never see them again. They know what it's like to be unable to hold a funeral, to grieve alone in your house because no one can come over to comfort you.

I feel like these new relationships are part of a continuum because my husband, Mike Mantell, was caring and friendly to everyone he met. The strength of his positive nature was even proved when our lives changed twenty years ago, when Mike was diagnosed with leukemia. He never turned negative, despite years of chemo and all that the disease entails. He was fortunate to be able to receive a bone marrow transplant from a relative, but he recognized how many—particularly members of Black and Hispanic communities—are not as lucky as he was to receive the procedure. So he designed a database for the Transit Authority to organize for bone marrow matches. And if someone was also diagnosed, he became their advocate and mentor. He believed in a community helping its own. And that is what I now do too.

## II. Wanderer

Coming from a large family with modest financial means, most holidays growing up seemed to resemble the Griswolds'—chaotic, with five young children crammed into the back of the family station wagon, luggage perilously strapped to the roof. Excruciatingly long journeys were only made longer as my distracted father drank in the bucolic landscape. "Dad, watch the road!" we screamed as his eyes lingered on another cornfield.

My father was an aimless wanderer by nature and an avid history reader. Most of our beach and pool holidays were actually historical sightseeing trips in disguise. One trip I recall where my father was in his glory was Charleston. He slowly ambled through the cobblestone streets, admiring the pastel-colored, pre-Civil War houses, stopping to read every historical inscription.

Looking back, I have now come to realize that my father possessed an uncanny gift. He had an innate stillness that allowed him to disentangle himself from the madness of society. My father didn't need a phone or camera to capture what he did on holiday like most rushed tourists who are afraid of missing out. Instead, he carefully wandered, gazing at the mundane to the magnificent. As I pass through rolling hills in the English countryside or simply a field of corn, I find myself looking through the lens of my father's eyes, and I smile, for in that brief moment, I can see the beauty in the ordinary just as he taught me so many years ago.

### III. Family Story

One Christmas years ago, Mike gave each of our five daughters large Buzz Lightyear dolls, though they were long past childhood. The girls were mystified at first about the meaning behind the gift, but they came to see how the gesture of Buzz pointing upward was symbolic of their dad wanting them to reach for the stars, to grab the unattainable and live meaningful lives. He wanted his daughters to soar. We still have two of the dolls, though I don't know where the others are—no doubt lost somewhere between the dorms of yesteryear and multiple moves.

I think about how furious I was then about the cost of the dolls, yet the memory has become one of our family legend stories. "To infinity and beyond!" We still say it, thinking of Mike, who was there for everyone throughout his whole life. But when he was sick and dying of COVID in Hackensack Hospital, he was alone. After he passed, they let me in to have an hour with him. What I was struck by as I walked through the hospital was the eerie silence. All the doors were closed. It was as if an apocalypse had occurred, the hallways as deserted as the streets outside.

Prior to when I'd arrived there, twenty minutes before Mike died, he FaceTimed with our daughter Mary Michael, and he was able to see his new granddaughter Penelope. I know that connection, however brief and tragic, exemplifies who Mike Mantell was. And I know that because of him—though she will not remember that moment—Penelope will reach for the stars too.

# WHEN I LEARNED GINA HAD DIED

Mera Cossey Corlett

*Mera Cossey Corlett lost her friend, Gina Hillman Allen, to COVID on November 8, 2020.*

I suspected Gina had good china. Just as I do. We were small-town, Western Kentucky brides in the eighties, where one received place settings from your registry little by little. Given at receptions with tables donned in white linen, pastel sherbet floating in the punch. A teacup here, a saucer or salad plate there, an entire place setting! As Gina's condition kept worsening, I kept wondering about that china.

For a stitch of time, we were hopeful. Chest X-rays showed change for the better. Her blood pressure was more stable. She was breathing on her own *some* over the ventilator. Her family seemed faintly optimistic, calling any trace of progress a "baby step." She was far from out of the woods. Still, all who knew her, who loved her, stretched for any morsel of forward movement.

In truth, none of us should have been surprised when it wasn't enough. Although she was always a fierce fighter, greater strides were needed to fracture COVID's fetters. But I understand why we allowed ourselves hope. All those little signs of forward movement fortified our faith and gave us something to cling to.

We were little girls in church together, Gina and I. Canton Baptist, a white clapboard country church on a grassy hillside overlooking the Cumberland. She was younger than me. Bright eyes, friendly, funny—the kind of girl Trigg County is proud to turn out. My vocation took me away to the city, and Gina's kept her there. I became a reverend, she a realtor. Social media allowed us to connect again.

Little reveals the irony of COVID as does Facebook. One day, on her Facebook page filled with photographs of grandchildren, Gina made a post about a lavish, over-the-top closet she'd seen. Two days later, a post said Gina had COVID. We all prayed hard, tugged on God's sleeve till our arms grew tired. My prayers were empathic since the virus had been my own adversary just months before.

I knew its face. The coughing, labored breathing, shortness of breath. Early fevers inducing teeth-chattering chills. Headaches, fatigue, body aches. Sore throat, congestion, runny nose. My hands tingled and my feet prickled, making me think of my extremities as a highway of electrical currents. The gloaming in my brain made me feel strangely off-balance—in body, mind, and spirit. And the dreams—vivid, visceral nightmares.

My daughter cried when I told her my test results, knowing what the diagnosis meant for those with preexisting conditions, and I have lupus. We prayed over the phone. I am a pastor; praying across airwaves is a common act (and preferable for quarantine). Some days, I didn't get out of bed except to sit in a chair, hoping to thwart pneumonia. To breathe, I slept straight as an arrow against the headboard. I told my family where I had hidden away valuables. I chose funeral hymns for fear that I wouldn't improve. I wrestled with pallbearer choices, sent out messages of love. I wanted nothing left unspoken.

By the grace of God and the mercy of modern medicine, I made it. COVID left its marks on me, but I am still here. And

Gina is gone. It is an enigma I cannot work out that fuels my survivor guilt, a common and much-studied experience following trauma where others have perished. Working through grief, I'm told the night terrors may dissipate. But I suspect one is never really the same after deciding which friends will carry your casket.

As a grief professional and pastor, I realize that trauma can be transformative and grief can be our teacher. Recognizing our hours and days are limited can free us to appreciate, like Emily in Thornton Wilder's *Our Town*, "every, every minute." The sun on my back. The touch of a baby's hand wrapped around my finger. I am more thankful, particularly grateful for my memories of loved ones like Gina who have already moved into the Mystery of Resurrection.

When they died, each of my parents left a bureau drawer filled to the brim with gifts they'd been given. Leather billfolds and Case pocketknives. Colognes and perfumes, each one still in its box, saved for "someday." My sister-in-law died suddenly from pancreatic cancer. Some forty years after she married, her bridal registry dishes and stemware remain packed in boxes in her grandparents' attic. COVID convinced me to stop living like that. I am using my good china, literally and figuratively.

It's like this: presently, my grandson, Henlee, is only a few months old. As much as I wish, I know I may never live to host his graduation dinner, his diploma laid next to his place at the table. But realizing that fact informs my life. Maybe in a little while, he and I may pull out the fancy bone china on some Tuesday evening when an autumn sunset has been particularly spectacular—the cheeky sun hanging on the horizon, bands of color painting the skyline. Who knows? We may pull out the good china even when the sunset is fairly standard. Because when you think about it, any ordinary sunset is extraordinary.

# EMPTYING HIS POCKETS

MARLENE BANDFIELD AND DAVID BANDFIELD

*Marlene Bandfield lost her brother, John Frederick Fischer, to COVID on April 11, 2020.*

## I. My Brother, the Collector

When my brother Johnny, a year younger than I, was a young child, he used to collect an assortment of bugs in various containers and in his pockets, which I'd always try to empty before our mother did the laundry. His collections evolved through the years to glass, rocks, and shells we would find along all the Long Island beaches we would frequent together. Later, he would collect baseball cards, comic books, coins, stamps, and flower and plant seeds for growing.

Johnny, a gentle and kind soul, died early in the pandemic, having contracted COVID in a nursing home where he was a short-term patient. He was my only sibling. We were fourteen months apart, and there was never a time in my life that Johnny was not there. I've lost a big part of myself as we were like Irish twins. I always protected my little brother, and I feel as though I failed him.

It took me over two years to be brave enough to go through all his collections. What do I sell and what do I keep? Why am I doing this? Where did Johnny go? He would want me to find the purpose and meaning in these questions.

## II. Of Flowers and Peppers

My brother-in-law's gardening efforts were exceeded only

by his generosity in giving away its bounty: peppers green, red, sweet, and hot. Tomatoes red, yellow, and purple, in astonishing quantity given the small strips of garden he grew them in. Square-foot gardening in tiny spaces between the house and driveway and along the fence, a vegetable high-rise of bamboo and wooden stakes supporting a backyard grocery store. Saving seeds, over the years he cultured his plants to love soil enriched with coffee grounds and eggshells from his job as a cook for Catholic Charities. And the flowers. The front of the house wrapped in a riot of impatiens and his darling, the stately pale-blue-flowered Monk's Hood backed by a white fence and attended by a carpet of yellow mums so striking that passersby would ask, "What *are* those?" All suddenly gone now but for the perennial Monk's Hood insisting we recall the splendor Johnny created for so many and how much we lost.

### III. The Bridge is Love

As teenagers, my brother and I enjoyed reading the same novels, and I vividly recall when we studied Thornton Wilder in English class. In Johnny's room, after he passed, I found *The Bridge of San Luis Rey* on a bookshelf and rediscovered the line, "there is a land of the living and a land of the dead, and the bridge is love, the only survival, the only meaning." Reading these words in his room, I felt that Johnny was talking to me. I thought back on that class so long ago and how we'd learned about another bridge that connects where humanity began and where it might go.

Then, in my brother's night table drawer, I found another book—one that my mother had bought for us when we went to see *How the West Was Won*. We saw this epic MGM Western with our parents when I was nine years old and Johnny was eight.

A family saga covering several decades of westward expansion in the nineteenth century, the movie ignited our lifelong love for Westerns. Originally filmed in three-lens Cinerama, and projected onto enormous, curved screens, the film was the grandparent of IMAX, and we were all absolutely amazed.

Johnny and I both thought the score was magic, and I remember how we enjoyed Debbie Reynolds singing "A Home in the Meadow." The song was set to the tune of "Greensleeves," our father's favorite melody, and since I took piano lessons, I kept playing the music for a long time afterward. Johnny loved hearing it and the adapted lyrics too. When I try to imagine Johnny in the world beyond this world, I hear the lyrics of the chorus beckoning us to a land full of hope. I remember us as children in that giant theatre, where we are *still* sitting beside each other.

# DUE TO COMPLICATIONS

Stephanie Wolf

*Stephanie Wolf lost her father, Herbert L. Wolf, on May 11, 2021.*

I have a memory card. 16 GB. It's in my closet downstairs, still in the audio recorder that I haven't touched since April 2021.

I remember some of what's on that drive. My father's recollections of his time in the US Air Force—he served four years at the Wright-Patterson Air Force Base near Dayton, Ohio, supporting troops overseas as a part of the Air Force Logistics Command. He talked about working in banking and shared a few memories of his parents, both immigrants from Eastern Europe. My dad loved to crack jokes, so there are plenty of cheesy punchlines on that memory card, along with his faint laughter.

My sister and I rushed to Florida in April 2021, me driving down from Louisville, Kentucky, and her grabbing a flight from Denver. Our dad had been battling aggressive cancer for years. So we had been here before. A panicked phone call from my mother to say Dad had a setback/fall/isn't doing well. Hurriedly making arrangements to head their way. But on our final day in Florida *that* spring, when my sister and I pushed back our departure time and decided to make one more visit to our parents' house, we took a photo: my mom, sister, and me surrounding my father in his hospice bed. I felt torn up saying goodbye then. I had a sense this would be the last time.

Herbert L. Wolf died on May 11, 2021, at the age of eighty-one. Cause of death: cancer. After four years of knowing this moment would likely come, and even having the peace of mind that he was no longer miserable and in pain, I still felt surprisingly unprepared for how to cope—those feelings further complicated by the pandemic.

We didn't hold shiva, at least not formally. My mother wanted to wait till everyone had the chance to get fully vaccinated before bringing us all together. It all felt rather unceremonious and strange, but I'll also never know whether having a more formal mourning process closer to his death would have helped me grieve.

My dad's death shook me, but the pandemic, of course, caused so much other chaos. We'd moved to Louisville just five days after much of the city had shut down, and I suddenly became a pandemic reporter, which felt impossible at times. Then, a few months later, I became a protest reporter, covering the historic racial justice demonstrations in the city. I delayed processing the things I had heard and witnessed because it felt like the best coping mechanism. So when my father died, I again delayed my grief, or at least tried to.

When we did go to Florida for a memorial service—that brief window when vaccines were widely available and the delta variant was not yet making headlines—I don't remember crying much, though I did cry a little at the cemetery. I kept busy coordinating with relatives, arranging bagel and lox trays, sorting through old photos.

In the time since his memorial, I feel like my grief has leaked out in bits here and there, sometimes without provocation or warning. There was a Kol Nidre service in Munich, where the nostalgia of the familiar hymns, the sense of resilience on grounds where our ancestors were once persecuted, and it being the first High Holidays without my dad, had me weeping the entire service, grateful for the face mask that hid some of my tears. There were the virtual work meetings where I suddenly felt overwhelmed by sadness and turned off my camera to hide. There was the one-year anniversary of his death, when my grief was less tearful and instead manifested as a foul mood and social isolation.

I think I'm still putting off processing so many of the experiences I've had or witnessed the past few years, still putting off fully confronting my grief. And if I'm being honest with myself, my grief isn't just about the loss of a loved one. It's about the anxiety of getting through each day during a global pandemic. It's about trying to find community in a new city where our first introduction to everything and everyone was through a computer screen. Because of my job, it's about having to ask other people about their trauma and grief. Mourning my father's death was another thing that COVID took hold of.

Shortly after my dad died, a colleague who had lost a parent told me the grief "doesn't go away but it does get gentler." So maybe when it's gentler, when all of it is gentler, I'll be ready to listen to that memory card from April 2021.

# HE KNEW WE WERE THERE

KATIE KEENE

*Katie Keene lost her father, Larry Keene, to COVID just after Easter Sunday, in April 2020.*

My father, Larry Keene, carried a quote around in his wallet: "A bell's not a bell till you ring it—A song's not a song till you sing it—Love in your heart wasn't put there to stay—Love isn't love till you give it away." Dad lived these words every single day and gave his love unselfishly, patiently, and unendingly.

And so, in honor of my dad's patience, we waited two and a half years to have his memorial service. Our decision to postpone was partially due to state social distancing mandates but also due to our own rules—my brother and I both have young children and another was on the way. As a family, we became determined to keep COVID from hurting anyone else we loved.

I don't regret this decision to delay his funeral. Our families are happy and healthy, and having the distance of time has allowed my memories of my father to come together in my mind again so I remember him separate from COVID and the Parkinson's and dementia that blurred our perceptions of him toward the end of his life.

From my first memories of him, Dad was my safe place. Calm and kind, big hugs and prickly kisses, he was never shy about hugging, kissing, ruffling hair, holding hands, dancing with me, or telling people how he felt. He never wanted to miss a minute and was an artist at transforming ordinary moments, like driving us to school in the mornings. Sometimes, he'd surprise us by stopping at the gas station down the street for a Little Debbie Sticky Bun. If it was cold out and the windows were fogged on the side, he'd take his ice scraper and sculpt a smiley face on my window. It's an image I will always treasure, in the same way I remember waking up one December morning at college and finding a freshly cut Christmas tree on my front porch. My father had cut the tree down for me and driven two hours just to deliver it. He didn't knock so he wouldn't wake me up, and then he went home. That's how he was. He never needed recognition for doing nice things.

A craftsman of daily life, my dad also made physical things and made them expertly. He loved teaching us what he knew, and what he had often already taught himself from books, back before internet instructional videos. He built our home almost entirely, taught us how to create stained glass windows, tile a bathroom, change oil, and catch our dinner, but he also showed us how to speak up for what is right and how to be good to people.

A fact of the pandemic is that the virus separated us all just when we needed each other most, though I have come to realize that we were one of the luckier families of COVID victims. While it hurt to not be able to touch him or be in his room at the hospice, at least we got to see my dad through the window. We were outside on the patio and he was visible to us through the glass door. The kids visited on Easter Sunday in their Easter clothes, holding up baskets and blowing him kisses. Knowing he was unconscious and that the thick exterior glass was between us, I still would talk to him anyway. I knew that his heart heard everything I said to him. I am 100 percent positive he knew we were there.

He fought much longer than the doctors thought he would, and at one point, a nurse suggested to my mother that it might be because we were there so much. I started to wonder if it was like he couldn't rest because, even unconscious, he still didn't want to miss a minute. The Thursday after Easter Sunday, my mom and I went there toward the evening. After sitting for a few hours, it was getting late, and I had to get the kids ready for bed, so I told my dad goodnight through the glass and left.

Mom stayed until after sunset, which had been vibrant and orange. Once the sun was going down low behind her, casting her shadow on my dad in his bed, it occurred to her that perhaps she could *hold his hand* in this way, with her shadow. She moved to where the sun cast her hand's shadow exactly onto his hand and sat like that, holding him until the sun went down.

She came home and told me this story, and two hours later, we got the call that my dad had passed. It felt so real, she said, as if she really had been holding his hand. It makes me so proud of my dad, who often stood silently yet defiantly against wrongs, that even as COVID was taking him from this world, he refused to go until he had that connection with us again.

Years ago, when I'd be leaving after a visit to go back to college, my dad would go out and stand in the driveway, waving until my car was out of sight (he did that for the rest of his life, in the capacity he was able, for all our departures). I'd like to think that having his memorial a few years after that spring sunset has at least given us the gift of perspective, enabled us to honor and emulate his enormous capacity for love rather than focusing on COVID. We are all in the driveway now, waving goodbye and remembering, and we will not stop.

# TILL YOUR BROTHERS
# OR YOUR SISTERS COME

Debra McCoskey-Reisert

*Debra McCoskey-Reisert lost her brother Bobby McCoskey to COVID on April 29, 2020, and her mother, Roberta McCoskey, to COVID on August 6, 2022.*

## A Man with a Heart

Our dear Bobby had a habit of contacting family members, beginning with, "Hey, don't tell Mom, but I took her phone. I wanted to call you." That was how those conversations would always start. And we deeply treasured those calls from him.

Robert McCoskey was kind, thoughtful, and always a little bit goofy, and he chose to spend his life giving back to the world. Every winter, he rang the Salvation Army bell outside stores, consistently bringing in the most donations. He helped out in food and toy drives too, wearing his Santa Claus outfit. That's how we'd like the world to remember Bobby, a real-life Santa, because he carried joy in his heart and his heart on his sleeve.

His good deeds didn't stop there, though. In fact, they didn't seem to stop anywhere. He volunteered at church drives and yard sales where he was known to give the shirt off his back, literally. Always a man for funny hats and good times, you can mention his name across the country and someone will pipe up to ask how he's been. Then they'll tell you a story from some beach or party many years ago. Always helping and lending a hand. It may have been while ringing a bell, riding his bike, or wiping the floor with you at the bowling alley where he showed his world-class skills, which were validated when he won a silver medal in the Special Olympics.

Such a kind man will have a good seat in the kingdom of heaven. Rest in peace, Bobby, and may heaven have a lane reserved for you. In our hearts, we will always be waiting for your phone calls. We will keep your secret, and we won't tell Mom.

## She Left Behind Her Faith, Hope, Love

Mom taught us many lessons. Most importantly is to have faith, hope, and love. She was the most complicated woman anyone ever met. Not that we needed a reminder, but she often said, "There's not another one like me." She was right. Mom was dealt a tough hand in life and was forced to be both our mother and father. She raised all six of us by herself.

God knows we were tough to raise, but she never gave up on us. She knew us thoroughly, knew our secrets, and never once broke our trust. A devout Catholic, Mom made sure we were at mass every Sunday, but she had a unique way of attending. She arrived late, but in time for the collection plate, and sat in the back of the church. This way, she could receive communion, listen just a bit longer, then beat the priest out the door. If she missed confession, she did not take communion. Especially if she'd thought about killing someone that week. Our mother was a good and faithful servant.

## Closing Time

One of our last trips together was to Tunica, Mississippi. We'd met to play at the casino because Bobby loved the slot machines. One night, it got late, so we decided to go back to the hotel. Once there, we knocked on Mom's door and took off running.

Mom got mad at us for making noise. The angrier she got, the funnier it was. We were making happy mayhem, and then we were lectured by our mother. We were all laughing so hard in the hallway—it was almost like we were little kids again.

No matter where he went or what he did, Bobby brought joy, like at dances he'd attend organized specifically for people with disabilities. Bobby fit in very well there. It was a place that he could go, have a really good time, be accepted. Once he was even crowned prom king. We all know Semisonic's song "Closing Time" that's played when bars close up—well, it's played at the end of those dances too. The lyrics always make me think of Bobby, in heaven, waiting for his four brothers and me, his little sister. No matter where I am, when I hear the song, I cry.

# BOBBIE LEE

## Jennifer Sullivan

*Jennifer Sullivan lost her mother, Bobbie Lee, to COVID on August 24, 2020.*

We were a musical family. My mom embarrassed me many times when I was a kid by singing and dancing down the grocery store aisles, and we'd been known to break out into harmonies singing ABBA's "Dancing Queen" in the car. Mom loved everything from Roger Whitaker to George Strait to Blondie, and her favorite song was John Denver's "Take Me Home, Country Roads."

My mom, Bobbie Lee, was diagnosed with Alzheimer's from a traumatic brain injury in the summer of 2014, and in late 2018, I had to put her in memory care. What a wonderful coincidence that this memory care had an accordion man named Joe, who played the "golden oldies" every Saturday afternoon for an hour. Those music days were a must for me.

It didn't take long for Joe to realize that "Take Me Home, Country Roads" was my mom's favorite song, so he played it every week, and my mom and I belted it out. I loved watching her eyes light up. She would sing and clap her hands, and sometimes, she would get up and shuffle around the floor.

When she sat back down, Mom would reach over and run her fingers through my hair and grab my hand and say, "You're so beautiful." I would always answer with, "You're so beautiful, too, Mom." And then we would go back to singing.

We did that for just over a year. As her Alzheimer's progressed, lyrics were almost the only words Mom had left. She had a hard time speaking, but when that accordion played, my mom knew all the words to every song. What a gift those Saturdays were!

And then COVID came and her memory care was closed. There was no music and no accordion man, and I could only visit with my mom through a window. She was confused and sometimes angry that I couldn't come in, but I would say, "There's a bad flu going around, Mom, and I don't want you to get sick." And for a moment she would remember. We went months and months like that, stuck on opposite sides of a pane of glass.

In July 2020, my mom turned eighty-two years old, and our family decided to have the best pandemic birthday party ever, and so we invited the accordion man to play at the window. We set up a shade tent outside by the dining room, we ordered pizza, and I made a cake so we could celebrate with my mom. She sat there in her wheelchair, bent over at the waist, eating and looking out the open window to see us, even though we were all wearing masks. And then Joe walked up and said, "Hi, Bobbie. I'm here to play for your birthday." He started playing the oldies, and suddenly, all the windows were open and the other residents crowded around, pressing their ears to the screens and clapping along. As his last song, Joe played "Take Me Home, Country Roads." Mom sang every word as I cried and watched the magic of music reach inside her and pull out her memories.

My mom got COVID just a month later and passed away on August 24, 2020. When Joe found out, he took to Facebook, singing "Take Me Home, Country Roads" for my mom, and wished her Godspeed. And now I am here with the memories of my mom and her life and our last precious years together. I know someday those country roads are going to take me home to her.

# Part II:
## Give Sorrow Words: How to Write about Who We've Lost

# LOVE LETTERS

My husband, Ray, who I knew for more than forty-two years, died of COVID in November 2020. I miss him every day.

When I met him, we lived eight hundred miles apart, so we wrote letters to each other. There was no internet or social media. We saved every letter and card we sent to one another—over 225 in all were written during the seven months we dated and were engaged.

After I lost Ray to COVID, I spent several hours rereading every word in those letters. What a beautiful reminder of our love back then that truly lasted through the years we had together.

My heart is forever his.

—Evelyn Richard

# GETTING STARTED: WRITING ABOUT LOSS

The motto of the WhoWeLost Project is "Shelter Their Story" because we believe that the lives of those we've lost to the COVID pandemic must be remembered and documented in a safe, welcoming place where comments and judgments are never allowed to enter. We encourage everyone to visit WhoWeLost.org again and again—to read, to write, to share. Each story submitted then keeps company with kindred spirits.

It is well established that writing is restorative in the grieving process, but if your intent is to memorialize someone you've lost, writing can become emotionally complicated, adding to feelings of loneliness and frustration. You know you want to do this, but how? Where to begin?

What follows is a series of general writing advice and some writing prompts designed to quietly spark memories and sustain your creativity as you try to write about someone you may have lost. Try reading all the way through this section first. Take some notes, and see what personally resonates with you before fully launching in. No single prompt will work for everyone, and what inspires you in a particular moment can, and often will, change. We hope you'll return to this brief, portable writing guide regularly—when there's a holiday, a birthday, or perhaps just when a gold-red autumn sunset brings forth a memory and makes you realize it's a good time to write.

Our aim with the Who We Lost Project is to restore the art of writing stories, in honor of our loved ones, creating narratives built from the beauty and importance of detail. When you're looking to begin a new piece of writing, one useful way to start is by setting up a structure.

You might fear that a guide like this could constrict your creativity—hindering the free flow of ideas and memories—but actually, the opposite is true. Many who have lost someone to COVID, or those who had a loved one die of other causes during the pandemic, express that they feel untethered and angry because so many people don't understand the unique grieving space they've been forced into. Plans and outlines can offer comfort because they ground us—stories may arise unpredictably from within you at any time, but your new writing structures, habits, and practices can be your constant, and consistent, companions. Grow comfortable with these ideas, and stories will become easier and more fulfilling to write. Of course, some of us bristle at the suggestion of structure, and in that case, we encourage you simply to write. The prompts are always here for you, if and when you decide you need them.

Here are a few, more general things to keep in mind as you set out to put pen to paper.

## 1) The Only Grammar That Matters Is Memory

Give yourself permission to forget before you remember. Five-paragraph essays and thesis statements are not relevant here. Ignore the echoes of your English textbook from forty years ago. Make notes in scrambled half-sentences, and ignore punctuation if you need to. Just getting the materials of your memories down on paper is what's most important. Later, if you want to share or publish your stories, that's the time to tinker with grammar and edit rough spots, if desired. You will notice that many of our prompt cues are phrased as questions, but the responses are just for you, to enrich your writing. Think of it as talking to yourself or singing in the shower.

## 2) Be Specific, Make Lists

There is no such thing as writing a story incorrectly. But there's one key element that will make the story you write particularly unique and meaningful: being specific.

Of course, there's nothing wrong with saying, "I miss my dad," but that doesn't describe *who* he was or *what* you miss about him exactly. Perhaps he loved Springsteen and sang "Born in the USA" loudly in the car. Maybe he had six sisters or put ketchup on his nachos, much to your disgust. Perhaps he helped you with your algebra homework even when he was exhausted after coming home late from work. Maybe he sometimes smelled a bit like pot after he went for a walk alone on the beach. Describing details like these—diving into those specifics that really *defined* your loved one—will help bring your memories to life on the page.

But how do you begin when there is abundant grief and so much to remember? It's impractical to expect you'll write your loved one's full life story; initially, focusing on one or two memories is much more manageable. And one way to start that process is simply by compiling lists: words, phrases, sayings. What's in your head at the moment? Jot it down. No need for complete sentences. Or find a thesaurus and make yourself a private word bank of language to draw from of anything that relates to the stories you're trying to tell. Often, one word will lead you to another, which will spark more ideas, perhaps taking you to places—new memories, new insights—you hadn't anticipated.

### 3) Titles Are Doorways

Titles do a lot of work. Think of them as doorways into your story. So, as you begin writing, it's sometimes helpful to start with a list of five potential titles. You may use all of them, or none. You might find that you need to quickly come up with five more. Allow yourself to play with language and consider what might happen if and when an unexpected door opens. Be sure to keep these lists—a title that wasn't useful for one story about remembering a fortieth anniversary party might be perfect for another story about traveling with your abuela on a Christmas trip.

### 4) Set Aside Your Device, Read Aloud to Yourself

Try to ditch your devices while you write, and reserve contemplative time to devote solely to your work. If your cell phone is pinging with notifications and texts, you can't focus your attention on your ideas. Write on paper, with a pencil or pen. It might feel odd at first, particularly if you only tend to work on a keyboard. Also recommended: get a loose-leaf binder. It's good to flip through your pages, to move and shuffle notes and lists. With a binder, everything stays in one place, and if you're feeling anxious and adrift, organizing your thoughts in this way can be therapeutic.

Also, make a habit of reading your work aloud to yourself, whether or not you feel a story is "done." The act of speaking your written words aloud is a gift. It will help you hear patterns, rhythms, and it will frequently spark more ideas to explore.

## 5) The Triptych, a Form Everyone Can Try

A triptych is an artwork made up of three pieces or panels. Often used to create a sequence or to show different elements of the same subject matter, triptychs are great structures for organizing and strengthening a story.

If you're percolating several small stories in your head but aren't sure how to connect them all, the triptych can be your friend. Just by being grouped together, the pieces automatically become a unit. Subtle patterns will begin to emerge. You'll think of more triptychs to try. It's magical. Here are some potential ways to think about the content of your stories in three elegant parts:

- Before, During, After
- Beginning, Middle, End
- Three Different Years, Seasons, Holidays, or Events
- Three Views of the Same Person at Different Points in Their Life
- Three Tiers of a *Día de los Muertos Offrenda* (Altar)
- Three Photographs
- Three Seemingly Separate Memories

This list, of course, is just a beginning, and there are many other avenues to explore, but coming up with an initial structure like this can help guide your thinking and lead you to new and interesting discoveries.

## 6) What Was Left Unsaid

Without funerals, memorials, wakes, and shivas, many of the stories we would have recounted about our loved ones are still waiting to be shared. Maybe you heard funny or poignant anecdotes at a

Zoom memorial or via a Facebook post, but those were transitory moments. This is why collecting stories with others, and recreating the social aspects of mourning that were forbidden for so long during the COVID pandemic, can be restorative.

Organizing the composition of a group story lets you direct a personal memorial, a structure to shelter your memories. So be the story gatherer. Try to enlist traditional family groups, families of choice, friend families, colleague and coworker families, or club and team members. It's useful to introduce this project at a holiday or social event where you can describe your purpose. It's a respectful way to remember who's not there and lets you focus attention on a positive activity rather than getting lost in the sadness of obvious absence.

If an in-person gathering is not an option, send emails and make calls explaining your goals. Suggest stories that share memories about your loved one specifically, using the prompts included here. Encourage recounting joyous memories, favorite moments, jokes, and shared experiences. Be direct: ask them to go beyond, "He was a great guy who will forever be missed." Push them to be specific.

Once you've collected the stories, take some time to sort through them all. Consider it a working document you can add to at any time. Take pleasure in the varied voices of your friends and loved ones. Let the stories flow organically because it *will* all cohere in the end.

And in the future, when you gather again with those who contributed stories, share them by reading aloud. Ask friends and family to read sections they didn't write; it's powerful to voice someone else's words. By the end, you'll have created a new tradition to repeat and be proud of.

# PROMPTS

Sometimes, it can be daunting to begin writing when faced with a blank page or screen. This is true for everyone—both experienced and beginning writers—and it's why writing prompts are popular, useful tools. What follows are prompts designed to spark memories and ideas. Think of them as starting points. You need not answer all the questions or stick to any prompt strictly; go in whatever direction works best for you. Combine the prompts or try composing small sections and then mixing up their order. Play and let your writing become a pleasurable, satisfying activity. Writing to remember and honor memories is a gift that comes from within you. Accept the gift.

## Prompt 1: Recipes, Remembered Meals

Specific food traditions are often inseparable parts of our individual and family heritage. A story inspired by a recipe or a memorable meal can evoke a time and place, honor culture and history, and also be literally useful—a recipe can be saved, referenced, followed, *and* enjoyed. Think back on those foods that have mattered to you, a dinner you long to eat that your loved one often cooked. Honor what they worked so hard to perfect. For example, you could write about an abuela's *arroz con pollo*, a sister's cornbread, or a husband's famous grilled skewers for the Fourth of July.

Some questions to consider as you write:

- What is the recipe or dish you wish to write about? What was simmering in your loved one's pots or baking in their ovens? Include it in the body of your story.

- For how long was this recipe or dish a part of your loved one's life? Was it handed down by other family members? Did you discover it together? Was it something you made together for special occasions or was it an important staple?

- What was the cooking process like? Who would be there? Where did it happen? What were the sounds, smells, and sights in the kitchen as the dish cooked? Did you help the chef? Did you chop and dice and stir? What kind of stories and jokes were told during this time?

- When the dish was ready, where and when was it eaten? How have you made or followed the recipe since your loved one passed? Will you keep up the tradition? Why or why not?

## Prompt 2: Lore, Legends

Remember the story your grandfather repeated about how he was rowing on the Ohio River when a storm came up out of nowhere and he thought he'd drown? Or the time your aunt ran into Paul Newman at a desert gas station in New Mexico? Everyone has their private lore and legends, stories that get repeated as if on automatic replay. Sometimes we tire of the repetition, but these stories have great meaning, so consider documenting them as a way to honor memories. Maybe write several and group them together, including family legends that may not be true.

Some questions to consider as you write:

- How did the story originate? Is it your mother's story? Is it passed down from her great-grandmother? But where did the story actually begin?

- When/where/why would the story be told? What would be the trigger? Did the story get told regularly at holiday gatherings? Did it always come out at a certain time of day or year?

- How would others react when they heard the story? Was there amazement, fatigue, anger, boredom, disbelief? Write out the story as best as you can remember it.

- Use a first-person point of view, writing in your loved one's voice. For example, "It was summer, 1939, and I remember seeing zeppelins flying over our backyard in Queens." Don't forget to be as specific as you can be!

- Or, be the narrator. For example, "I loved sitting with my Grandpa when he'd tell me stories about his childhood. One of his favorites was about zeppelins, floating through the blue skies in Queens."

- Consider the context. Why was the story so important to the storyteller? If you know the history, wouldn't it be wonderful to preserve? Or ponder the backstory and guess—this is what writer's do, filling in what's forgotten and unknown.

## PROMPT 3: OUR MUSIC

There is copious research addressing the intricacies of how music affects the brain. But you don't need to be a neuroscientist to appreciate the connections between memory and music. You know this instinctively—when you're driving and a song comes on the radio, sending you back to senior prom, or a first wedding dance, or childhood vacations at the shore. Your brother's 1980 garage band attempting Pink Floyd's "Another Brick in the Wall." You might sing along and it feels like time travel. Nothing else mimics this experience.

Because music helps you tap into your deepest emotions, in times of grief, specific songs support connections to your loved one. Allow yourself this pleasure, the conjuring of time and place, even though it's bittersweet. Seek the music that has meaning to you, and let it inspire your stories.

Some questions to consider as you write:

- There are many ways that music can enter your writing, so consider: What are some of your favorite songs? What music made your loved one happy or sad? What songs you did share?

- What are some personal stories associated with this beloved music? A favorite composer, artist, album, concert? Did your loved one enjoy karaoke? What was their signature tune? Did they play music as they drove or did yard work or plodded on a treadmill?

- Include some (or all) of the lyrics from songs in your stories. Let those words enrich the story you have to tell. Or, let the lyrics be the story.

- Try a triptych story. Write about three different songs, and you will find that they'll all mesh together effortlessly. Or write about the same song, recollected in three different settings, as a way to evoke the passage of time.

## PROMPT 4: LETTERS

We all have moments that make us wish we could communicate something to the person we've lost. Some might accomplish this through prayer, some of us just speak our thoughts aloud in the moment—"I wish you could see me fixing this sump pump, Dad," or, "Mom, look at your granddaughter's flapper Halloween costume."

Another way to express the emotions behind these stories is by literally writing a letter, or a series of them, directly to your loved one. In literature, this is called an "epistolary" form. Try this technique, and you'll be participating in a long tradition of direct address to those we miss the most.

Some questions to consider as you write:

- Try using a second-person voice: address your writing to a "you." This conveys a sense of immediacy and privacy.

- Don't be afraid to state what it is you need and want to say. No one needs to see these letters unless you want them to.

- Consider establishing a ritual. Write on Diwali, Thanksgiving, Ramadan, Hanukkah, birthdays, anniversaries, etc.

- Try this as a family (defined broadly . . . friend and work families matter too). Ask family members to contribute a letter, then gather the results together. Add to the group portrait when and if it's appropriate.

## Prompt 5: Ephemera and Their Favorite Things

We all have possessions that may or may not have monetary value but that bring us security, comfort, and delight. These *favorite* things are the perfect jumping off point for a story because they are often imbued with personal history and meaning.

This might be a useful writing focus if you're tasked with clearing out the home of someone you've lost and come across their ephemera. (A common definition, descended from ancient Greek, is "the minor transient documents of everyday life.") Examples of ephemera include grocery lists, recipes, "notes to self" such as Post-its, newspaper clippings, postcards, greeting cards, airport destination tags, blank checks, ticket stubs, menus, receipts, sheet music, and calendars. When gathered together, ephemera can describe a precious life.

Giving yourself a creative goal can color the mood and be a help to *you*, the person excavating and packing. Create one designated box of things and resolve to write stories about what you've gathered. Take your time. Maybe just work on one small story per month. In this way, a simple cardboard container becomes a treasure chest, and the items it holds feel less burdensome.

Some questions to consider as you write:

- Describe the object. Does it have an origin story? Did someone save it up for years? Was it handed down through generations? Purchased on a vacation? Found on a fishing trip?

- Think broadly about your subjects. Your dad's prized '57 Corvette would be a cool story because it's iconic, but so might his worn plaid flannel shirt that you took from his closet because of all the memories it evokes.

- Who will keep the object now? How do you feel about that? Do you want it?

- Most of us have several favorite things, so try writing about three items without attempting to connect the separate narratives. These were all possessions of your loved one, so they're inherently linked.

- What is the ephemera you want to write about? What is its meaning? Does it signal something unique about your loved one? Does it mark a particular point in your loved one's life?

- Consider preserving ephemera by quoting documents verbatim to integrate into the story. This honors quirkiness and ushers the loved one's voice into the narrative. Or you can even let the document be the story. As is. Found art.

## Prompt 6: From a Photo

Our phones have made us into accidental archivists and curators of our own lives, and they can be an excellent database for stories. Writing about a photo might seem like it's easy, but we've become so used to snapping pictures all the time that it will be rewarding to coax a story out of your images, especially because taking a photograph can affect your recollection of a moment or event.

It's essential to look back further than the recent past of your phone and wander through whatever albums of pictures you're fortunate enough to possess. This is restorative, though it can be difficult—a perfect companion to your writing process.

Some possible questions to consider as you write:

- Write a story in three sections about three photographs (a triptych). Give each section a different title.

- Title the stories in a way that conveys the context of the photograph. For example, use titles like, "Plum Beach, Fall Break, 1983," "Dad's Sixtieth Surprise Birthday Party," or "Jessie, at Home."

- Write about the photograph how you would talk about it.

- Imagine you're describing the photo to a person who cannot see it. Who's in it? Where and when was it taken? Does there seem to be a special occasion that inspired the picture to be shot? Are there details in the background that speak to time and place—a *Día de Los Muertos* altar? Uncle Jay's tackle box? Aunt Sarah's convertible?

- Ask several people to write about the same photo. Everyone may have different recollections and points of view about it. It will make for an interesting story!

- Ask family and friends to cull through their photos and contribute a narrative of their own choosing. They will appreciate the opportunity to be a part of the remembrance you're composing because they are also grieving this loss.

## Prompt 7: Dreams

At the outset of the pandemic, there was an abundance of news stories about dreams that seemed to be spurred by quarantine and social isolation—surreal and hyperreal nightmares that occurred frequently and tended to linger throughout the day. Much was made of the phenomenon, partly because it allowed us to contemplate the seemingly benign terrors coming from within us in the midst of the actual, petrifying unknown.

Several years later, news reports of "pandemic dreams" have disappeared, but the WhoWeLost Project regularly receives dream stories. Many people are still having frantic nightmares, overflowing with imagery so vivid it feels electrically charged. And depending upon one's own point of view and/or religious and cultural beliefs, the phenomenon is looked upon in varied ways. Some are comforted by these dreams and feel they've been visited by their loved one. Others, particularly those who live with PTSD, may be "reexperiencing" traumatic pandemic events, and this prompt might need to be discussed with a mental health professional before being attempted.

Interestingly, some writers want to publish their dream stories right away, as if to banish it from their system, but others ask that we hold onto them until they're ready to let others see such personal work. So we encourage you to record your dreams and see how it feels, or try integrating a dream into one of the stories you write. It can feel quite liberating to commit the dream to the page, either attempting to interpret the meaning, or just leaving it be.

## PROMPT 8: DAWN, DUSK, DETAILS

Whether you're writing stories about your own life or remembering your lost loved ones, it's vital to see that no subject is insignificant or trivial. Sometimes the smallest detail says the most. Everything can be celebrated, yearned for, and mourned. So, leave openings to be inspired by.

Here are some potential ideas to consider:

- Nature: The change of seasons, time of day, and weather events.

- What Remains: Memories that call to us at any point, on any day. Missed calls and texts, a glance from a stranger, lingering scents, an overheard conversation, a few bars of a song.

- Sports: Allegiance to a favorite team can define and bring meaning to a fan's life. What did it mean to your loved one? Who will watch and attend the games now that they're gone? Are there fan traditions that will be carried on in their memory?

- Pets: The dog still waiting near the door at a certain time of day is a devastating image. If there was a pet in the life of your lost loved one, don't forget to write about them. If the pet brings you comfort, they deserve your attention on the page as well as on your couch.

- Fun: What was your loved one's favorite, oft-repeated joke? How about TV shows and movies? What did you watch together? What games did you play together and love?

## PROMPT 9: WHEN A LIST IS THE STORY

The act of making a list can be the foundation of a story. Sometimes, though, the list itself *is* a story, or perhaps an accidental poem that will surprise and inspire you. This is a good story form to try with a group or if you're including children in your writing circle. Begin with one main idea and then jot down what comes after. Embrace sentence fragments and incomplete thoughts. If a phrase doesn't seem to fit, leave it and keep going. You can always edit or add something later.

This is a good form to repeat on holidays or milestone events and celebrations. It is very inclusive because usually everyone can contribute. Be the scribe and then read the completed list-story back to the people who offered their memories and observations.

A few suggestions to kick off a list story:

- So far, you have missed . . .

- I/we miss . . .

- Things in [your loved one's] junk drawer . . .

- What [a loved one] kept in her purse . . .

- I wish I had told you . . .

- He/she/they loved to cook . . .

- On our vacation, we . . .

- We will never forget when . . .

- I miss hearing you say . . .

# BIBLIOGRAPHY

Bogost, Ian. "The Age of Social Media Is Ending." *The Atlantic*, Nov. 10, 2022.

Boss, Pauline. *The Myth of Closure: Ambiguous Loss in a Time of Pandemic and Change*. New York: W. W. Norton & Company, 2022.

Cha, Ariana Eunjung and Dan Keating. "COVID Becomes Plague of Elderly, Reviving Debate over 'Acceptable Loss.'" *The Washington Post*, Nov. 28, 2022.

DeSalvo, Louise. *Writing as a Way of Healing: How Telling Our Stories Transforms Our Lives*. Boston: Beacon Press, 2000.

Handler, Jessica. *Braving the Fire: A Guide to Writing about Grief and Loss*. New York: St. Martin's Griffin, 2013.

Harris, Mark. "Imagining a Memorial to an Unimaginable Number of COVID Deaths." *The New York Times Style Magazine*, Nov. 9, 2022.

Kübler-Ross, Elisabeth and David Kessler, et al. *On Grief and Grieving: Finding the Meaning of Grief Through the Five Stages of Loss*. New York: Scribner, 2014.

Levin, Dan. "They Died from COVID. Then the Online Attacks Started." *New York Times*, Nov. 27, 2021.

Pennebaker, James W. and Joshua M. Smyth. *Opening Up by Writing it Down*, Third edition. New York: The Guilford Press, 2016.

Pennebaker, James W. and John F Evans. *Expressive Writing: Words that Heal*. New Bedford, Indiana: Idyll Arbor, 2014.

Pinsky, Robert. *The Sounds of Poetry, a Brief Guide*. New York: Farrar, Straus and Giroux, 1998.

Pinsky, Robert and Maggie Dietz. *Americans' Favorite Poems: The Favorite Poem Project Anthology*. New York: W. W. Norton & Company, 1999.

Sholtis, Brett. "When COVID Deaths Are Dismissed or Stigmatized, Grief Is Mixed with Shame and Anger." NPR "Here and Now": August 30, 2021. https://www.npr.org/sections/health-shots/2021/08/30/1011785899/when-covid-deaths-are-dismissed-or-stigmatized-grief-is-mixed-with-shame-and-ang

Smith, Clint. "Monuments to the Unthinkable." *The Atlantic*, November 2022.

Stolberg, Sheryl Gay. "A Lasting Legacy of COVID: Far-Right Platforms Spreading Health Myths." *The New York Times*, Nov. 22, 2022.

Wagner, Sarah E. *What Remains: Bringing America's Missing Home from the Vietnam War*. Cambridge: Harvard University Press, 2019.

Wakin, Daniel J. "'Those We've Lost,' a Chronicle of COVID Death, Comes to a Halt." *The New York Times*: June 4, 2021.

Yong, Ed. "The Final Pandemic Betrayal." *The Atlantic*, April 13, 2022.

Young, James E. *The Stages of Memory: Reflections on Memorial Art, Loss, and the Spaces Between*. Amherst: University of Massachusetts Press, 2016.

# CONTRIBUTORS

**Dawn Sizemore Adams** is a family nurse practitioner in urgent care. After losing her father to COVID, she founded Live Like Pop: The Penny Project, a memorial that honors people lost to the virus. The project features pairing coins with stories as a way to evoke Dawn's childhood memories of her father's laundry business. She lives in Alabama with her husband and son.

**Pamela Addison** is the widow of Martin Addison, who lost his life to COVID at the start of the pandemic, when her children were just five months and two years old. Since Martin's death, she has become a COVID loss advocate, focusing on the young children who have lost a parent or caregiver. In November 2020, she founded the group Young Widows and Widowers of COVID-19 to help others feel less alone on this unexpected and difficult journey of love, loss, and grief. She hopes her story can make a difference and create change, especially for the youngest victims of this pandemic, the children.

**Mina Aguilera** was born and raised in Texas. She has two sons, Michael and Julius, and a granddaughter named Mia. Her husband, Cesar Velasquez, died due to COVID on July 9, 2020. They were married for twenty-six years.

**Mark Aldrich**, a one-time winner of the New York Press Association's annual award for Best Humor Column, is a writer and occasional performer who lives in New Paltz, New York.

He has worked as a writer in formats that include journalism, technical documentation, audio theater, and sketch comedy, all of which can be found at his website, TheGadAboutTown.com.

**David Bandfield** worked for over four decades in broadcast television. He enjoys volunteering for his community, gardening, reading and spending time with his family, especially his three-year-old granddaughter.

**Marlene Bandfield** was born in the Bronx and grew up on Long Island, New York. Marlene worked as a physical therapist for forty-two years and is now retired. She lives in northern New Jersey and takes cares of her granddaughter and mother. She enjoys reading, cooking, traveling, and being engaged with her standard poodles.

**Jessica Bostwick** is a teacher in New Jersey. She is the proud daughter of Polish immigrants, Stanislaw and Barbara Bury. Jessica lost her father to COVID on January 6, 2022. Jessica and her husband, Keith, welcomed their son, Anthony, in November 2022. They will continue to share all of the wonderful memories they have of Tata with him.

**Sheri Clark**, PhD, is a licensed psychologist in the states of Arizona and North Carolina. She is originally from Huntsville, Alabama, and received her doctorate in counseling psychology from the University of Tennessee-Knoxville. Prior to relocating to Arizona, she was a staff psychologist and an associate director/director of training for the Counseling and Psychological Services Center at Appalachian State University in Boone, North Carolina.

**Mera Cossey Corlett**, a pastor, chaplain, counselor, and poet, has centered her vocation around ministry to those experiencing grief and loss. Born and brought up in Cadiz, Kentucky, she moved to Louisville to attend seminary, fell in love with the city, and stayed. Presently, she is senior pastor at Okolona Baptist Church. When she is not writing sermons, Mera enjoys being with her husband, Kevin, and her family, particularly her precocious grandson, Henlee.

**Rosie Davis** was born in California and currently resides in Texas. She is married and has two daughters and a son. When Rosie lost her mother to COVID in May 2020, she put her grief into action and started the Yellow Heart Memorial to honor the lives lost to the virus. Rosie is on a mission to leave a legacy and humanize the numbers.

**Catherine Wright Flores** has been writing and creating since she could climb into a backyard tree with a stack of her dad's old work papers to flip over and excitedly scribble stories on at age seven. She lives in the Houston, Texas, area with her husband, Marc, and their two children, Amelia and Luka. She is the founder of a nonprofit, Scarf Therapy, in memory of her brave mom, and she is currently honoring both her mom and dad with an in-progress work about tending to the magic in our midst while surviving loss.

**Bob Greenberg** is an actor-comic who regularly performs standup at the Friars and Gotham Comedy Club. He has been featured on *SNL, Conan,* and *Letterman* and has had roles on *Law & Order* and *The Characters*. His film credits include *Tango Shalom* and *A Very Merry Toy Store*. He starred as "Morty" in the national tour of *Old Jews Telling Jokes*. He is a die-hard New Yorker.

**Camille Gregorian** has enjoyed a long career in clinical social work in hospital settings, primarily in leadership positions. After cutting back to part-time work in 2019, she rekindled her interest in art and is now an emerging, intuitive, abstract painter. She also volunteers her time with a local Armenian Historical Museum and enjoys traveling and learning about new cultures. Camille lives and works in Rhode Island.

**Dawn Hamilton** resides in Indiana with her husband and two rescued brindle dogs. She enjoys her role as Mom to three and Grammy to six. The written word has always been easier for her to express her thoughts than conversing. Her mother, **Ruth Ann Trobe**, has the heart of a nurturer and initiates conversations with strangers to both their surprise and delight; she is a mother, grandma, great-grandma and until recently, the love of a very dear man.

**Diane Hawkins** is a communications coordinator at the Louisville Metro Department of Public Health and Wellness. The Chicago native has worked as a copy editor at several newspapers, including the *Chicago Sun-Times, Courier-Journal*, and *Milwaukee Journal Sentinel*. She is a proud member of the National Association of Black Journalists and Alpha Kappa Alpha Sorority, Inc.

**Max Hoffman** is an anesthesiologist and critical care physician at Brigham and Women's hospital in Boston. He completed his residency at NYU Langone Medical Center, where he served as chief resident before completing a fellowship in critical care medicine at Duke University Hospital.

**Susanne Howe**, after an early career in health care marketing and grant writing, made the transition to a profession in senior care. Specializing in life enrichment and activities, she has worked in assisted living and home care for the last fourteen years. She has been the activity coordinator for the health care and rehabilitation center at Treyton Oak Towers in Louisville, Kentucky.

**Laura Jesmer,** LCSW, is originally from the suburbs of Chicago and received her masters of social work degree from the University of Illinois, Urbana-Champaign. Ms. Jesmer is a psychotherapist in private practice in the Phoenix area who specializes in trauma healing and personal growth. Prior to opening her private practice full time, she served as the clinical director at Arizona State University's counseling services.

**Katie Keene** is a teacher and has three wonderful children. She is passionate about nature—so much so that during COVID quarantine, she began a flower farm on the eight acres that she grew up on. She is proud that she gets to raise her children in the same house that her dad built.

**Ed Koenig** lives in New York City. Retired from a career in information systems, Ed is now exploring other interests, including music and writing. He has found great solace in sharing stories on WhoWeLost.org of his partner of thirty-three years, Jody, who died from COVID-19 in April 2020. Ed is currently working on a memoir with the working title of *At the Intersection of Life and History*, where he explores his acknowledgement of his sexual orientation, his personal relationships, and his connection to many of the events that make up the history of the movement for LGBTQ+ equality.

**Kim Kuperschmid** is a singer, musician, recording engineer, and business owner who lives on Long Island with her husband, both of their children, a cat, and a dog. She was raised in a two-family home in Floral Park, New York, and was blessed to have grown up with loving, supportive parents and maternal grandparents.

**Pablo Lopez Jr.** is a United States Army Veteran. He was born and raised in Brooklyn, New York, to parents of Puerto Rican descent. He served in Germany and deployed to Kosovo with NATO and during the Iraq War of 2003. After leaving the military, Pablo's focus has been on giving back to the veterans' community by working with nonprofits. He served as the New York State Yellow Heart memorial team lead.

**Mary Mantell** met her husband, Mike, when they were students at Pace University, and they were married for thirty-eight years. Their five daughters are Brittany, Katarina, Alexandria, Mary Michael, and Jennie. Mary volunteered extensively throughout their childhoods, including being a Girl Scout leader and PTA member. She currently works in sales merchandising and lives in New Jersey.

**Alexandria Mantell** is a vice president at HPS Investment Partners LLC. She received a MPhil in finance at University of Cambridge, UK, and a BA in applied mathematics at Barnard College, Columbia University. Alexandria grew up in River

Edge, New Jersey, with four rambunctious sisters and now currently resides in London with her two children and husband.

**Kimberley Martin** has worked remotely since 2007 and is currently the associate dean of colleges and curriculum at a nationwide university. Her husband's death upended her life and led her down new creative paths to cope with the grief and pain of a significant pandemic loss. Kimberley is located in a rural wooded area of mid-Missouri and thrives by being immersed in nature—a love she shared with her late husband and hopes to pass on to her only grandchild, Hogan.

**Clara Martinez** is a grieving mother. Both of her children, Donovan Kittell and Stephani Kittell, were born on Halloween, three years apart. Donovan passed away at thirty-one from COVID. Clara lives in southern California with her husband.

**Debra McCoskey-Reisert** resides in Florida. She is married and the mother of two grown sons. She founded an organization called Bobby's Bikes, which works within communities to provide children with less resources the freedom and happiness of riding their own bikes, to carry on her brother Bobby's good spirit of love and generosity. Debra is active in many COVID advocacy and memorial groups.

**Nicholas Montemarano** is the author of three novels, a book of short stories, and *If There Are Any Heavens*, a memoir about the loss of his mother to COVID. He teaches creative writing at Franklin and Marshall College.

**Rebecca Pape** is a cardiothoracic ICU travel nurse and an Army veteran. She is trained in heart and lung bypass life support and has cared for the sickest patients under the last option of life support. She lives in Pittsburgh, Pennsylvania, with her two cats.

**Ti Spiller Phillips** thinks it is better to be kind than to be smart. She prefers animals to humans and trusts neither anymore.

**Evelyn Richard** was raised in a very small town in Kentucky but was lucky to meet a man from Massachusetts "who swept me off my feet." Evelyn and Ray lived in Massachusetts for ten years and then returned to Kentucky. Evelyn has two fine sons and the blessing of five amazing grandchildren. Evelyn and Ray's wonderful life together was cut short when Ray Richard died of COVID-19 on November 14, 2020.

**Rima Samman** was born in Beirut, Lebanon, and immigrated to the US with her family in 1989. After graduating from college, she worked in leadership positions in the retail industry and in the field of eye surgery. When her brother Rami died, and Rima designed the Rami's Heart COVID-19 Memorial, her aesthetic and photographic skills were reignited. Rima's artistry, which springs from grief, propelled her—along with her partner, Travis Whitaker—to create the first permanent physical COVID memorial in the United States (https://www.ramisheartcovidmemorial.org/). Its presence provides comfort and healing to thousands of the COVID-bereaved.

**Rachael Sandoval's** father was in the Navy, so her childhood was spent being bounced around all over the United States. She settled in Ohio and had six children. For well over a decade, she was a single mom, working third shift and sometimes two jobs to provide. There have been hurdles and heartbreak, but there has also been fierce determination and happiness. Rachael says she was once asked, "Who are you?" and responded, "I am Rachael. I am a mom." But looking back at it now, she believes she would answer, "I am a soul living a human experience. One day I will be reunited not only with my son but with all my loved ones."

**Krishna Sankaran**, MD, a nephrologist, grew up in the Chicago suburbs. He has practiced in Rockford, Illinois, since 1992 and is now a professor of medicine at his alma mater, UIC College of Medicine. He married his sweetheart, Mary Sankaran, a nurse he met when he was a medical student. They raised four children, three of whom work in health care. In a few years, he hopes to retire and teach full time at UIC.

**Catherine Sasanov** is the author of three poetry collections and the libretto for the theater work *Las Horas de Belén: A Book of Hours*, commissioned by Mabou Mines. She is currently working on a nonfiction book, piecing together the lives and community of three people who murdered their enslaver in Charlestown, Massachusetts, in 1755. Her essay, "The Will, the Woman, and the Archive," reflecting on what it means to be a poet in the archive, can be found in the anthology *Slavery's Descendants* (Rutgers, 2019). She lives near Boston.

**Aszdáá Nizhónii Bit'ah níí (Carol Curley Begay Schumacher)**, is a proud member of Diné (Navajo Nation) and is originally from Arizona. Carol and her husband live in Sun Prairie, Wisconsin, and have six children. She is a first-generation college graduate from Herzing University. Carol works in the Madison Metropolitan Area School District, doing her life's work, as she started out taking care of kids and still takes care of and works with kids. She especially loves working with young ones and always shares her life stories, language, and culture with whoever shows interest or will listen.

**Mark Slaugh** is the oldest of five in the Slaugh family. He's an entrepreneur and advocate since the inception of the modern cannabis industry. Based out of Colorado, Mark has been involved in the poetry and spoken word community since 2011. His mother passed from COVID in 2021, and two of his siblings were shot in the Club Q incident in Colorado Springs. He hopes his contribution helps others heal from loss, pain, and suffering of their loved ones and to remind survivors that though they may be lost, they are never forgotten.

**Lisa Smid** is a freelance copywriter, editor, and communications consultant. Her poetry has been published in the *Belmont Literary Journal*. She has left New York and returned to her native Nashville. Her COVID awareness art projects include the social media hashtags #MaskHotMonday and #YellowHeartTuesday.

**Steven J. Stack**, MD, MBA is the commissioner for public health of the Commonwealth of Kentucky. Dr. Stack was appointed commissioner in February 2020 and was subsequently elected secretary-treasurer of the Association of State and Territorial Health Officials in the fall of 2020 and president-elect in 2022. He is a board-certified emergency physician with more than twenty years of emergency medicine clinical practice and emergency department management experience. Throughout his career, Dr. Stack has served in numerous medical professional association leadership roles. In 2006, he was the first board certified emergency physician ever elected to the American Medical Association Board of Trustees, and in 2015, he served as AMA president.

**Jennifer Sullivan** lives outside of Portland, Oregon. Her mother got COVID in an outbreak in her memory care unit and passed away in August 2020. To heal, Jennifer started a podcast, *For Those We Lost*, where she interviews others who have lost loved ones to COVID. You can find her at www.Forthosewelostpodcast.com.

**Jerri Vance** lives in Princeton, West Virginia. She has four children—Megan, Tyler, Julia, Jamie—and a grandson, Tucker. She is an active advocate, works with COVID Survivors for Change, and also helps administer the Facebook group Young Widows and Widowers of COVID-19. Her husband, James D. Vance, passed away on January 1, 2021.

**Jamar Wattley** is a registered nurse who specializes in critical care. Jamar has been involved in all aspects of COVID since the beginning, from administering monoclonals, giving vaccines, and caring for patients from med/surg to critical care status. He lives in Kentucky, is married, and has three boys. His wife, Bridget, also works in health care as a medical technician.

**Stephanie Wolf** is a public radio journalist whose work has aired on national programs like NPR's *Morning Edition, All Things Considered, Weekend Edition*, and *Here and Now*. She's also reported stories for PRI's *The World* and was a 2021 Arthur F. Burns fellow, spending two months covering culture and education issues in Germany. Prior to her career in journalism, Stephanie was a professional ballet dancer and had a twelve-year performance career with companies like the Minnesota Ballet, James Sewell Ballet, and Wonderbound, formerly Ballet Nouveau Colorado.

**Jacqueline H. Woodward** was the loving wife to Gary Woodward for forty-five years. She has three daughters, and is the "YaYa" to six grandchildren. She holds an MSW from Western Kentucky University and worked for the Kentucky Cabinet for Health and Family Services for over thirty years. She is currently a licensed administrator for Med Center Health. Her passion is to view others with a wide lens, love deeply, and always speak kindness to others because one never knows what someone else is going through.

# ACKNOWLEDGMENTS

I am often asked where this project comes from within me and why I persist to get it right.

Although the initial idea for the WhoWeLost Project originated while listening to a COVID update press conference in Kentucky, it took months of working on the initial website for me to comprehend that the essence of my inspiration was my father's death in 2009. An optometrist, my father went for a walk and was struck by a car whose driver had no peripheral vision due to undiagnosed brain tumors. He died alone on the pavement, and the image has been lodged in both my waking and dream life ever since. My father had remarried after my mother's death a decade earlier, and his old and new families did not get along. There was awful discord and lawsuits. My brother and I were excluded from shivas and collective mourning. There were no proper goodbyes.

And so, the trauma inherent in what it means to lose someone to COVID had already been part of my existence for the eleven years prior to the pandemic. The situations are not the same, but there are visceral parallels. My personal understanding of ambiguous loss and disenfranchised grief has informed every decision I've made about how to provide safe shelter for stories and memories of the COVID-bereaved. I feel protective of each story that is published on the website and every story present in this anthology. And I am grateful that the writers trust the project will keep watch over their memories. This anthology is not "mine"—it is a memorial, dedicated to the precious souls we have lost, and I am profoundly aware of my responsibility to honor them.

I have had conversations with many of the writers whose stories appear here, and I have corresponded with hundreds of those who have published stories on WhoWeLost.org. I thank all of them. Their opinions and insights are endlessly appreciated. They have changed my life and how I think. There are also many stories that *should* be present here but aren't due to space constrictions. This troubles me greatly; however, this anthology is part of the larger project, and I will persevere to feature these stories in other ways in the future.

This book couldn't exist without the exquisite team at Belt Publishing. I will be forever grateful to Anne Trubek, Belt's founder, publisher, and editor, who embraced this book and understood why it needed to exist. Thank you to Michael Jauchen for his sensitive editing expertise.

Thank you Laura Jesmer, LCSW, and Dr. Sheri Clark. Experienced trauma therapists, they undertook much of the research for a portion of the introduction and provided expertise, as well as their own personal insights about grief.

Thank you to Donna Jo Thorndale, who offers inspiration and vision; she is my tuning fork on all matters relating to this project. I am grateful to my poetry soulmate Catherine Sasanov, who has collaged ideas with me for three decades. Erin Keane is steadfast, wise, and innovative—thank you. For providing valuable feedback, especially in the earlier stages of this project, I am grateful to Dr. Julie Cerel, Kinsey Morrison, Dr. Gordon DeFriese, Carol Turner, Nancy Gall-Clayton, Emily Goodlett, Mary Rotella, Dr. Joe Rotella, Rima Samman, and Mary Wright. The support and advice shared by the WhoWeLost board of directors is necessary and appreciated: Steve Cambron, Juli Duvall, Jennifer Goldberg, Suzanne Powell, Dr. Amy Shah, Rabbi David Wirtschafter, and Joan Wojan. Board member Allison Lynn Jones passed away in October 2021, and we miss her every day.

I thank COVID Survivors for Change, particularly their COVIDconnections group led by Amy Stewart. The empathy and love demonstrated at each Thursday night session is remarkable. I am also grateful to our writing workshop—I am lucky to be your instructor.

Thank you to Sarah Wagner, professor of anthropology at George Washington University, whose friendship and insights have influenced my outlook about this entire project. Sarah and her students are working on "Rituals in the Making," a project on memorialization, misinformation, and the consequences of the COVID-19 pandemic. Their observations about WhoWeLost are astute, and I treasure their ideas.

I have been interviewed by several journalists in the past few years, and I've found that every conversation sharpened my focus and sometimes helped me make connections I may have otherwise missed. And so, for their brilliant questions, I am grateful to Ed Yong, Stephanie Wolf, Linda Blackford, Sheryl Gay Stolberg, and Dawne Gee. When Scott Gabriel Knowles asked me to be a guest on his live podcast, "COVIDCalls," any doubts I may have had about the project disappeared; his work has shaped international discussions of the pandemic, and I thank him for including me.

Thank you to Alan Lytle for producing and airing WhoWeLost stories on WUKY; it's vital that the stories are heard as well as read. Thank you to the Carnegie Center for Literacy and Learning, who generously let me teach workshops centered on writing and grief. I thank Alexander Taylor for his art that informs the aesthetics of the project, Patrick Elward for his technical expertise, Michael McClain for his legal acumen, and Art Greenwald for his brotherly nudges and firewall advice.

Finally, I could not have begun the WhoWeLost Project, or completed this book, without the support of my partner, Michael McWilliams, and my daughter, Lucy Biberman. Thank you for listening, supporting, schlepping, quarantining, masking, and sometimes crying with me. I love you.

The WhoWeLost Project is a 501(c)(3), and profits earned by the editor will be directed toward the continuing operating costs and maintenance of the organization.

# ABOUT THE EDITOR

Martha Greenwald is the founding director and curator of the WhoWeLost Project. Her first collection of poetry, *Other Prohibited Items*, was the winner of the Mississippi Review Poetry Series. She is the winner of the 2020 Yeats Prize. Her work has appeared in many journals, including *Poetry, New World Writing*, the *Threepenny Review, Slate*, and *Best New Poets*. She has held a Wallace Stegner Fellowship at Stanford and has been awarded fellowships from the North Carolina and Kentucky Arts Councils, the Breadloaf and Sewanee Writer's Conferences, Yaddo, and the Vermont Studio Center. A New Jersey native, she lives in Kentucky, where she taught English, creative writing, and ESL for eighteen years.

CPSIA information can be obtained
at www.ICGtesting.com
Printed in the USA
JSHW020931030623
42678JS00001B/2